Beyond Debt
The Greek Crisis in Context

NIKOS TSAFOS

CONTENTS

ACKNOWLEDGMENTS

Many people helped me think about the Greek and Eurozone crises by reading and commenting on my blog, Greek Default Watch, or by listening to my arguments over coffee, food or drinks. I have benefited immensely from the challenges that they have provided, helping me refine my own understanding of politics, economics and political economy. But mostly, I have benefited from my family and a close circle of friends, who have kept this crisis real for me, reminding me of the immense human toll that it has taken. This book is dedicated to them.

ABOUT THE AUTHOR

Nikos Tsafos has lived and worked in Greece and the United States, and his career spans the private, public and nonprofit sectors. As author of one of the few bilingual blogs on the Greek crisis (Greek Default Watch), he has written extensively on the roots and trajectory of the crisis since it started. Trained as an economist and political scientist, Tsafos holds a BA from Boston University and an MA from the Johns Hopkins School of Advanced International Studies.

INTRODUCTION

On May 5, 2010, the Greek parliament met to discuss a €110 billion loan that would allow the country to keep paying its bills, avoid default on its debts, and ensure its continued membership in the Eurozone. The proximate cause for the bailout was that Greece could no longer convince investors to lend it money at reasonable rates. To finance its needs in 2010 and 2011, the Greek government needed to borrow €128.7 billion, but high debt and large deficits made it harder to raise this money.[1] At year-end 2009, Greece's public debt stood at €298 billion, or 129% of its gross domestic product (GDP), and its budget deficit was €36.1 billion (15.6% of GDP)—both the highest in the Eurozone.[2] As a result, investors doubted that they would be paid back and demanded to be compensated for the extra risk of lending to a sovereign whose creditworthiness they questioned. In 2008, markets lent money to Greece for an annual yield of almost five percent; by April 2010, they demanded almost eight.[3] By itself, this meant an additional ~€2 billion annually on interest payments. It was too much, and so Greece negotiated a lifeline with a troika consisting of the International Monetary Fund (IMF), the European Central Bank (ECB), and the European Commission (EC).

One hundred thousand people gathered on May 5 to protest the proposed cuts in spending and the increases in taxes that the loan agreement entailed. Most protestors were peaceful. But a few blocks from the parliament, hooded men threw a Molotov cocktail into the office building of Marfin Bank. They attacked the twenty-four people who were working inside rather than heed the call for a nation-wide strike. Three of them died—among them a 32 year-old pregnant woman who was about to learn the sex of her child.[4] The economic crisis had taken its first victims. A few months later, in November 2010, one observer said of that tragedy:

> The deaths of three innocent employees shocked Greece, shifting the national mood and the course of this year's crisis. Instead of rising social unrest as many had feared, Greece has seen only fragmented opposition to the euro zone's most drastic austerity measures. An expected backlash against the ruling Socialist govern-ment failed to materialize in recent local elections. And last week, when the government announced fresh budg-et cuts, the streets were mostly quiet.[5]

The qualified optimism seemed justified. In August 2010, the IMF published its first assessment of Greece's progress, observing that:

> The program is off to an impressive start. This is fully in line with the high expectations expressed by the interna-tional community when agreeing to the extraordinary fi-nancial support package. A disappointment so far has been that, at this defining moment for Greece, the eco-nomic reforms have not had broader support from oth-

er political parties. While most of the difficult reforms still lie ahead, developments during this early phase of the program augur well for the government's determination to press ahead.[6]

In December, the IMF was still optimistic, although starting to worry about the pace of progress. Greece cut its budget deficit by an unprecedented amount in 2010. The IMF noted that, "the program is broadly on track, but at an important crossroads, where a second wave of fiscal adjustment and structural reforms needs to find traction, and where political resolve will be needed to overcome vested interests."[7] Its conclusion:

> The program is up to a very good start, but pressure points evident in the public sector, and still generally unfavorable investor sentiments, suggest that the program is at crossroads. Further fiscal adjustment and—above all—the return of robust economic growth hinges crucially on a strong determination on the part of the Government to forcefully advance its structural reform agenda in the coming months, in the public sector and more broadly. Such reforms will undoubtedly be fiercely resisted by entrenched vested interests, testing the government's resolve. But the Government's determination to date, together with a favorable political calendar, augurs well for the prospects in this regard.[8]

By July 2011, the IMF's enthusiasm was tempered as the reform momentum had fizzled. The IMF complained of "inertia" and urged Greece to "vigorously implement [new] policies in a timely manner."[9] A few weeks later, the European Union announced a second aid package to Greece, including €109 billion in fresh funds and a plan for the private sector to reduce its holdings of Greek debt by €50 billion.[10] In November 2011, as the country finalized the details of that second loan agreement, the Greek prime minister was forced to resign, paving the way for a caretaker government to hold elections.

As the country went to the polls, first in May 2012 and then again in June 2012, whatever optimism remained had evaporated. By June, the economy had been in recession for four years. Income had contracted by a fifth and GDP was lower than in 2002. Investment had halved.[11] Bank deposits had fallen by a third, as people moved money overseas or tapped into savings to survive.[12] Eight-hundred thousand people had lost their jobs—one in five males and one in four females could not find a job, and fewer than half the people aged 20—24 were employed. Employment in construction had almost halved, and it had shrunk by a third in manufacturing.[13] Compensation per employee had fallen by nine percent and prices had risen by a tenth due to higher taxes.[14] Health was deteriorating with suicides estimated to have risen 46% from 2007 to 2010, while "the Minister of Health reported a 40% rise in the first half of 2011 compared with the same period in 2010."[15] The deepening crisis decimated the political system. In the May 2012 elections, the party with the most votes won less than nineteen percent of the total, and the top two together got under thirty six percent. Only in 1950, when the country held its first election after a civil war, did the top two parties receive a similarly meager share of the vote. Another election would be needed. Greece was stuck.

■ ■

How did Greece become the epicenter of Europe's "existential crisis," as German Chancellor Angela Merkel called the Eurozone crisis, and why did the country need so much money in May 2010? Why did it choose this loan rather default or leave the Eurozone, as many said it should have? And why did Greece fail to recover by June 2012, needing a second bailout, holding successive elections and swearing in its fourth prime minister in a year? This book is an attempt to answer these three questions.

The answers offered were many: tax evasion, statism, corruption, populism, immigrants, too much spending, too little, austerity, clientelism, lawlessness, fake statistics, the PASOK party, the New Democracy party, Prime Minister Papandreou (Andreas and/or George), Prime Minister Kostas Karamanlis, the 2004 Athens Olympics, the European Union, the Eurozone, German Chancellor Angela Merkel, the IMF, the Americans, credit rating agencies, banks, speculators, military spending, capitalism. Everything went wrong. But "everything" was synonymous with "nothing." How important was each factor? What role did it play? Did it cause the crisis, affect its trajectory or complicate its resolution?

In their diagnoses, people focused too little on Greece and too much on debt. Paul Krugman, a Nobel laureate in economics, said Greece's internal problems were "beside the point" and that "the Greeks can't solve this crisis anyway."[16] Yanis Varoufakis, a Greek economist, believed that "there is no such thing" as "the Greek crisis."[17] According to this narrative, Greece was merely at the wrong place (Eurozone) at the wrong time (as the global economic crisis worsened). Of course, Greece was not alone, and its condition ought to be put in its international context. From September 2008, when Lehman Brothers went bust, through 2011, the IMF had offered aid to three Eurozone countries (Greece, Ireland, and Portugal), three EU members (Hungary, Romania, and Latvia), and other states such as Iceland and Ukraine. Bigger economies like Italy and Spain had come under severe pressure by investors. Yet the economic crisis did not affect everyone equally. The Eurozone included countries with growing economies and contracting economies. The crisis hit states with high debt levels and runaway finances (Greece and Italy) as well as countries with low debt levels and well-managed public finances (Ireland and Spain). This crisis was more than Greece but less than the Eurozone. If three people go out in the snow and only one catches a cold, you can only blame the snow for so much—something more is going on.

If people paid too little attention to Greece, they paid too much attention to debt. Debt became the barometer for the crisis, the lens through which to judge Greece's prospects. The economist Nouriel Roubini noted that Greece's debt level meant the country "is not just suffering from a liquidity crisis; it is facing an insolvency crisis too," and he recommended an "orderly default."[18] Mitt Romney, the Republican candidate for president in the 2012 US elections, kept attacking President Barack Obama for taking America on the "path to Greece." This obsession with debt was understandable—Greece had more debt relative to its economy than any other Eurozone country, and this debt would have to rise before it fell. But debt was a symptom, not the disease, and reneging on it would be a palliative, not a cure. There was a notable gap between diagnosis and cure. Analysts outlined the various problems facing Greece—tax evasion, excess spending, corruption, and overregulation—and then recommended default and devaluation. This was like giving aspirin to a person needing surgery.

■ ■

A close look at debt accumulation was revealing, however. Greece's debt to GDP ratio was 129% in 2009. This was its historical path:

1980: 22% of GDP.
1993: 99%.
2004: 99%.
2009: 129%.[19]

Over three-quarters of Greece's debt was thus accumulated before there was a Eurozone, and over four-fifths came in just two periods (1981—1993 and 2004—2009). Understanding "what happened in Greece" requires an analysis of those two periods, and understanding those periods also explains why the country found it so difficult to adjust after 2009. Telling that story means looking closely at the politics, economics and political economy of the last half century.

After the Second World War, Greece struggled to achieve prosperity and legitimacy at the same time. The economic growth of the post-war period did not lead to a corresponding expansion in political inclusiveness and participation—much of the electorate was alienated and a part of it was persecuted. The situation changed in the 1980s. The country's first socialist government brought into the mainstream a new class of citizens. But it did so by spending money it was unwilling and unable to raise and by extending its reach deeper into the economy, intervening and controlling more activities to serve political ends. Besides an explosion in public debt, mismanagement brought forth an economic crisis, political instability and successive elections in the late 1980s. At that point, the promise of entering the Eurozone provided an anchor, and at last, Greece had both legitimacy and prosperity, even if the prosperity barely compensated for the stagnation of the 1980s. Once in the Eurozone, the discipline waned and the budget balance turned negative. It turned even more negative after 2007, when the conservatives won their first reelection since 1977, paving the way for their longest stay in power since 1974—1981.[20] The conservatives went on a spending spree that mirrored the 1980s, spending lavishly on wages and pensions without raising taxes by a commensurate amount. And just like the first binge, it too ended in political and economic crisis.

In the 1990s, Europe had served as a catalyst for change by providing an endpoint (joining the Eurozone) that enjoyed cross-party consensus. In the first two years of the

Greek bailout, external help had made possible a sizeable fiscal consolidation driven by higher revenues and lower spending. But Greece was nowhere near an exit. Greece has neither prosperity nor legitimacy. To achieve prosperity, the socialist government needed to uproot the bonds of legitimacy that brought it to power. It could not do it, and it collapsed.

■ ■

As a political scientist and an economist, I have approached these three questions through a political economy lens—how changes in an economy affect politics and how politics affect the economy. As a Greek who lives overseas but who travels back to Greece often, I benefited from having both intimacy with and distance from the subject. Having grown up and lived in Greece, I understood the place, its rhythm and its logic; and living abroad allowed me to look at my country from afar, helping to avoid the noise of the daily news cycle and to focus on the deeper structures from which this crisis emerged. Primary information and statistics, flawed as they were at times, formed the backbone of my research. Writing a blog on the Greek crisis for over two years allowed me a real-time appraisal and reappraisal of the crisis, its roots and its trajectory.

In writing this book, I had three goals. I aimed, first, to be clear. This is a complicated crisis that straddled politics, economics, society, history, and philosophy. Telling the story required numbers, hard facts, and a delving into intangibles such as "fairness" or "legitimacy." So often, arguments get tangled, and hypothesis is presented as fact. Clear thinking and writing should help the reader to follow the story.

I aimed also to be concise. This is not the comprehensive history of the crisis. It does not chronicle every number or story that I found in my research, nor does it contain a billion numbers and charts. Relevance is my only yardstick—how can I best answer these questions: what happened in Greece; what could be done about it; and how did Greece fare?

I aimed, finally, to be balanced. Balanced does not mean neutral or equivocal, nor does it mean having no point of view. There is a clear and strong argument in these pages. But I tried to be fair and treat facts as facts. I was guided by George Orwell's retort: "We have now sunk to a depth at which the restatement of the obvious is the first duty of intelligent men."[21] Restatement is necessary in a deep crisis, and there is no sense in denying the obvious.

WHAT HAPPENED IN GREECE?

In the 1950s and 1960s, Greece was a poor, agricultural country recovering from war. It took fifteen years (1953) for GDP to reach its pre-war (1938) level.[1] Relative to the countries that would ultimately form the European Union (EU-15), per capita income was just half the average in 1960—only Spain and Portugal were poorer.[2] Almost sixty percent of Greece's population lived in rural areas, more than in any country save Portugal, and Greece's population was more rural than today's China or Egypt.[3] A third of the people were classified as illiterate in the 1951 census.[4] In 1960, agriculture "[accounted] for about one-third of the national income, [provided] employment for over half the population, and [supplied] about four-fifths of the country's total exports."[5] Infant mortality was twenty percent higher than the European average, trailing all countries except Portugal, and a Greek infant was almost three-times more likely to die at birth than an infant in Sweden.[6] Life expectancy too was below the European average.[7] Telephone penetration surpassed only Portugal and was almost two-thirds below the European average, lower than today's India or Zimbabwe.[8] Sixty percent of merchandise exports came from food, three times the European average and the highest share in Europe.[9] Tobacco, the most important exported good, yielded $72.4 million in 1960, while American aid brought in $56.4 million.[10] The state was modest: revenues were 21 percent of GDP in 1962—1964 against 28 percent in Europe.[11] In

1964, Greece had to contend with "considerable underemployment, the low incomes of a large section of the population, the worsening of the trade balance, and the slowness of industrialization."[12]

The Post-War Growth Miracle

Greece's economy was transformed after the war. Economic growth in the 1960s and 1970s was forty percent higher than the OECD average (6.6% versus 4.7% in 1961—1978).[13] Greece's economy in 1979 was four times larger than in 1953, while the urbanization wave was complete. Agriculture remained larger in Greece than elsewhere in Europe, but the gap was narrower. In 1980, per capita income was 7% below the EU-15 average on a purchasing power parity basis.[14] Greece had closed the gap based on an economic transformation with several features.

Urbanization. People from the countryside moved either overseas or to the major urban centers of Athens and Thessaloniki. In 1961—1981, the population of Athens grew by 68% and Thessaloniki 58%; as a result, 41% of all Greeks lived in these two cities, up from 28% in 1961.[15] But urbanization also meant uneven development as the cities grew faster than the countryside. In 1965, per capita income in Athens was fifty percent higher than the country-wide average and twice as high as that of Epirus, the poorest region.[16] By 1981, consumption in Athens was still fifty percent higher than in rural areas.[17] Athens had twice as many doctors and fifty percent more hospital beds per capita as the rest of the country—the gap was greater relative to poorer regions.[18] The growth of the cities created a widening gap with the countryside.

Agricultural modernization. Internal migration relieved the agricultural sector of excess labor and allowed it to grow as well. Crop production rose by 50% in the 1960s and 1970s and livestock grew by two-and-a-half times.[19] Agriculture was mechanized: the country had six times more tractors in

1980 than in 1961,[20] and yield per hectare for several crops doubled between 1961 and 1975.[21] Employment in agriculture almost halved, and real incomes rose by 4.1% a year in 1950—1975.[22] But this growth rate was slower than the national average of 6.2%.[23] In 1958, agriculture made up 26% of households' income; by 1980, it was 16%.[24] The city grew faster than the country.

Table 1—Greece: Economic Indicators

	1960	1970	1980	1990	2000	2010	Source
Population (000s)	8,332	8,793	9,643	10,157	10,917	11,316	1
% Urban	42.9	52.5	57.7	58.8	59.7	61.4	1
GDP (bn €2005)	33.15	74.86	117.34	125.65	158.38	193.75	2
GDP/capita €2005	3,979	8,513	12,169	12,371	14,507	17,123	2
GDP/capita EU=100	57.6	83.0	93.0	74.7	73.3	77.6	2
Value Added (%)							
Consumption	78.3	64.0	64.1	70.8	70.7	74.5	2
Gov't Spend	11.9	11.9	14.6	16.3	18.3	18.2	2
Investment	15.1	32.5	27.7	25.0	24.5	16.2	2
Exports	12.4	9.8	24.1	18.5	24.9	21.5	2
Imports	17.6	18.2	30.4	30.6	38.3	30.4	2
GDP (%)							
Agriculture	16.6	14.5	13.9	9.8	6.7	3.1	2
Industry	24.7	30.7	30.4	27.2	21.5	18.8	2
Services	58.7	54.8	55.7	63.0	71.8	78.0	2
Employment (%)							
Agriculture	53.8	40.5	30.8	24.5	16.7	11.4	3
Industry	18.1	25.6	28.9	27.4	20.1	18.8	3
Services	27.7	33.9	40.3	48.1	63.2	69.8	3
Gov't (% GDP)							
Expenditures	22.5	24.9	30.3	45.2	46.7	51.5	4
o/w interest	-0.9	0.4	1.4	9.0	7.4	5.9	4
Receipts	21.0	26.0	29.2	31.0	43.0	39.7	4
Public Debt		17.9	22.5	71.7	103.4	148.3	5

Sources: (1) World Development Indicators; (2) EC, AMECO, Updated 11 May 2012; (3) OECD (1960-1990), Eurostat (2000-2010); (4) OECD (1960-1980), Eurostat (1990), ELSTAT (2010); (5) EC, AMECO, Updated 11 May 2012 (1960-1990), ELSTAT (2000-2010).

Industrialization. The movement of people to the cities helped the country industrialize. Industrial production (excluding construction) grew by ten percent a year in the 1960s and by eight percent in the 1970s.[25] Industrial goods accounted for a quarter of all exports in 1975, up from less than one percent in 1954.[26] Lignite production rose seven-fold in 1960—1975, fueling a growth in mining.[27] But Greek manufacturing remained fragmented. In 1958, establishments that employed over 10 people accounted for a mere 1.6% of total employment, and more than half were one-man shops.[28] "According to the 1969 census of the industry and handicraft sector, enterprises employing less than 5 persons accounted for 41 per cent of total industrial employment and those employing less than 20 persons for nearly two-thirds."[29] And, "the proportion of the self-employed in total non-agricultural employment is close to 40 per cent, which is not only considerably above that of OECD countries of similar level of development but also above that of many developing countries outside the area."[30] This structure persisted, and in 1980, 41% of the people employed in "industrial establishments" worked in companies with fewer than ten people.[31] Besides hindering economies of scale, this dispersion also hampered efforts to boost tax collection, as transactions were harder to monitor in small establishments.

Monetary stability. Greece devalued its currency in 1953 and kept a fixed exchange rate of thirty drachmas to the dollar in the 1960s and early seventies. Faith in banking system attracted private deposits which rose fivefold between 1955 and 1960.[32] Change was quick: "In view of the hyperinflation in Greece during the Second World War, it is remarkable how a few years of financial stability sufficed to restore confidence in financial assets by around the end of the 1950s."[33] Besides providing a good environment for economic activity, the rise in deposits also made it easier to finance industrial activity[34] and public deficits.[35] The country abandoned its peg to the dollar in March 1975, but the depreciation to 37 drachmas per dollar in 1979 was modest (relative to what came next).[36] The country enjoyed low inflation in the 1960s (~2%) and not extreme inflation in the 1970s (when high inflation became a worldwide problem).

Sound public finances. The ordinary state budget, excluding public investment, was balanced in the 1950s—1970s. Public deficits tended to be small—around 1.5% of GDP—and the state had no trouble financing them from domestic savings and foreign capital. Deficit spending went to infrastructure, and from 1951 to 1975, the state covered thirty percent of all new investment, providing a vital supplement to the private sector and helping to generate economic growth both directly and indirectly.[37] But Greece did not follow the general trend of Western Europe, where economies redirected resources from military to civilian use. Military spending remained high, and Greece spent five to six percentage points of GDP on defense in the 1950s. That spending fell by one percentage point in the early 1960s, but it came up again. Throughout the 1970s, Greece ranked among the highest spenders in North Atlantic Treaty Organization (NATO).[38]

Investment, chiefly in housing. Between 1960 and 1973, investment contributed to half of the country's economic growth, and its importance rose from 15% to 43% to GDP.[39] Of that, housing was always the most important piece, making up 30% of all investment; buildings in general (not just dwellings) accounted for almost half the investment in 1958—1975.[40] This reliance on housing drove economic growth, allowed the country to absorb the massive urbanization drive towards Athens and Thessaloniki, and it rebuilt the stock that had been destroyed during the Second World War. It also created a new class of citizens, the rentier, for whom rents formed the primary source of income—around six percent of tax returns in 1970 listed rents as their primary income, a share that rose to almost eight percent by the early 1980s.[41] The reliance on housing, however, proved excessive: "During the sixties, the ratio of housing investment to fixed investment in manufacturing industry averaged 2.4:1 in Greece, compared with 0.6:1 in Portugal and Yugoslavia, 0.7:1 in Spain and 1:1 in Turkey."[42] The focus on housing created a bubble: new building activity was rising at fifteen percent a year in the decade before it peaked in 1974, causing inflationary pressures. Then the market crashed after the government introduced a number of measures in 1972 to curb the boom in housing.[43] A second boom-and-bust in the late 1970s triggered another recession.

Emigration. Around 1.3 million people emigrated from 1950 to September 1977, when Greece stopped collecting statistics as the number of emigrants had dropped to around twenty thousand a year.[44] Given a 1977 population of 9.3 million, the net outflow was enormous and carried several benefits. First, it offered another outlet besides Athens and Thessaloniki for people seeking employment, thus alleviating the pressure of under- and unemployment. Second, it provided a steady flow of foreign exchange. Remittances accounted for three and a half to four percent of GDP in the 1960s and early 1970s. Third, by providing foreign exchange, emigrants made it easier for the country to finance its current account deficits and maintain a fixed exchange rate with the dollar. And fourth, emigrants invested in Greece, chiefly in housing, aiding the most important driver of development in post-war Greece.

Tourism and shipping. In the 1960s, receipts from tourism and shipping grew by an annual rate of 14—15%. In the 1970s, the growth accelerated and shipping rose by 21% and tourism by 25% a year. Shipping surpassed remittances in 1974 and tourism surpassed them in 1978. The Greek-owned merchant fleet quadrupled from 1960 to 1980, and in 1980, Greek interests controlled 12% of the world's fleet.[45] In tourism, from four hundred thousand tourists in 1960, Greece received more than five million in 1980, a twelvefold increase.[46] In 1980, the country had five times as many hotel beds and twice as many hotels in operation.[47] But Greece lagged its peers in dollars earned per inhabitant, nights spent per hotel bed, nights spent overall, and tourism revenues as a share of GDP.[48]

Table 2—Greece: Invisibles Balance
in US$

Year	Total Invisibles	Shipping	Remittances	Tourism	EEC Transfers	Other
1965	549	164	207	108		71
1966	636	183	235	143		75
1967	659	214	232	127		86
1968	714	243	234	120		116
1969	788	244	277	149		118
1970	949	277	345	194		134
1971	1,292	369	470	305		148
1972	1,606	436	575	393		202
1973	2,195	600	735	515		345
1974	2,399	867	674	448		411
1975	2,725	845	782	644		455
1976	3,024	914	803	824		483
1977	3,497	1,127	925	981		465
1978	4,422	1,177	984	1,326		934
1979	5,662	1,519	1,137	1,662		1,344
1980	6,159	1,816	1,059	1,734		1,551
1981	6,482	1,826	1,057	1,881	148	1,569
1982	6,098	1,657	1,016	1,527	550	1,348
1983	5,529	1,309	912	1,176	834	1,299
1984	5,289	1,095	898	1,313	715	1,268
1985	5,261	1,039	775	1,428	869	1,150
1986	6,512	1,001	942	1,834	1,392	1,342
1987	8,567	1,193	1,334	2,268	1,666	2,106
1988	10,099	1,380	1,675	2,396	1,935	2,714
1989	10,281	1,375	1,350	1,976	2,602	2,979
1990	13,041	1,762	1,774	2,587	2,901	4,017
1991	15,354	1,774	2,115	2,567	4,034	4,863
1992	17,264	1,993	2,366	3,272	4,058	5,575
1993	17,023	1,920	2,360	3,335	4,085	5,323
1994	18,767	1,957	2,576	3,905	4,307	6,022
1995	20,770	2,190	2,982	4,136	4,968	6,495

Source: ELSTAT, Statistical Yearbook, various

Insular economy. Greece was not an export-oriented economy. In the 1960s, exports accounted for about 11% of GDP, a share that rose to 15% in the 1970s. Nor were exports sophisticated: "The commodity composition of Greek exports remains [in 1971] relatively unfavourable. Although substantial progress has been made in recent years in developing exports of industrial goods, food and agricultural materials still provide more than one half of total exports."[49] In 1970, "Greek manufacturing industry has remained heavily dependent on the domestic market … nearly three-fourths of manufacturing industry was overwhelmingly to the extent of 80 per cent or more oriented to the home market."[50] Foreign direct investment (FDI) was also minimal, "totalling about $620 million or $250 million net of capital repayments and profit and interest payments for the entire period 1954 to 1976."[51] In one year alone (1975), Greece attracted more from remittances than it did in foreign investment throughout the twenty years prior. At its highest, Greece took in $672 million in 1980 from FDI—this is relative to $1 billion in remittances and $1.8 billion each from shipping and tourism.[52] Foreign investment was driven by Greeks living abroad—foreign direct investment did not matter.

Economic Growth, but Political Stagnation

Economic growth brought neither political normalcy nor legitimacy. Political participation and institutionalization lagged behind economic development, the country's politics remained contentious, and the political system was unable to accommodate the aspirations of an increasingly affluent society. It was a problem that Samuel Huntington articulated in his seminal book *Political Order in Changing Societies*:

> Social and economic change—urbanization, increases in literacy and education, industrialization, mass media expansion—extend political consciousness, multiply political demands, broaden political participation. These

changes undermine traditional sources of political authority and traditional political institutions; they enormously complicate the problems of creating new bases of political association and new political institutions combining legitimacy and effectiveness. The rates of social mobilization and the expansion of political participation are high; the rates of political organization and institutionalization are low. The result is political instability and disorder.[53]

One result was frequent elections. From 1946 until a military junta took power in April 21, 1967, Greece had twenty-one different prime ministers (many were caretaker governments), and the country changed leaders twenty-eight times.[54] Greece held nine parliamentary elections in that time—one every 816 days (two years and three months). In sum, thirty-one parties entered parliament in those nine elections. But two-thirds of those parties only entered parliament once and then either disappeared or merged with other parties. Another six entered parliament twice, all in successive elections. Of the thirty-one parties that made it into the legislature, only three entered parliament more than twice (four times each).[55] The political system was thus fragmented, representation was weak, and power was dispersed. In part, this was the norm in Greece. Emmanouil Roidis, a Greek satirist, wrote in 1875, "Elsewhere parties come into existence because people disagree with each other, each wanting different things. In Greece, the exact opposite occurs: what causes parties to come into existence and compete with each other is the admirable accord with which they all want the same thing: to be fed at the public expense."[56] Rather than reflect ideology or sectional interests, parties were personalized, ephemeral, and thus, easily created and disbanded. Constantine Karamanlis, who served as Greece's prime minister, offered a similar assessment in 1966: "Parties are formed more to satisfy ambition and interests rather than to express ideas and popular trends. They are formed and disbanded, they cooperate and intertwine with such sloppiness that the people can hardly follow their multiple incarnations."[57]

But political weakness was both the cause and the consequence of irreconcilable politics. As the Nazis left Greece in October 1944, the country started to be embroiled in a civil war that lasted from 1946 to 1949. The civil war was the product of tensions between the communists, a political force whose influence was growing, and the royalists, which represented the traditional political elites and which enjoyed the support of both the British and, then, the Americans:

> The Greek crisis of 1946—1949 has to be viewed as the result of a Communist-inspired revolution domestically conceived. That is how the leaders of the insurgency viewed their struggle at the time, generally labeling it a people's revolution (*laiki epanastasi*) whose ultimate goal, a people's democracy (*laiki demokratia*), would be the first major step on the road to true 'socialism' (i.e. communism).[58]

Even before the Second World War, the communists had become a potent political force, receiving almost ten percent of the vote in the June 1935 elections (but no deputies) and six percent of the vote in 1936 (their fifteen deputies held the balance in parliament). Their rising power alarmed the country's conservative forces, including the monarch, who had been restored to power in 1935 after an eleven-year absence. Growing unrest culminated in May 1936 during a strike by tobacco workers in Thessaloniki that turned bloody with twelve people killed. Ioannis Metaxas, appointed caretaker prime minister during a political stalemate, "was able to play on the seeming inability of the politicians to compose their differences and on the serious labor troubles to predispose the king to accept his proposals for a 'strong' government."[59] Arguing that an upcoming 24-hour strike would be the first step to the communists taking power, he succeeded in convincing the monarch to suspend parts of the constitution and establish a military dictatorship on August 4, 1936.

The Metaxas dictatorship "had little difficulty in neutralizing such opposition as existed,"[60] and "most of the KKE [Communist Party of Greece] leadership was quickly jailed."[61] The communists were thus weakened during Metaxas's rule. But after the Axis occupied Greece in April 1941, the communists formed the backbone of the resistance to the foreign occupiers. Their appeal was based on calls for national liberation and socioeconomic reorganization rather than communist revolution.[62] As the political elites fled to form a government in exile, the communists expanded their reach: "through example, discipline and propaganda they were able to offer a vision of a better and just future that was quite beyond the politicians, whose old antagonisms appeared irrelevant in the misery of the occupation."[63] By contrast, the "leaders of the old political parties rejected the communists' call for co-operation and stood largely aloof from the resistance struggle."[64]

As the Axis retreated in October 1944, there was bound to be tension between the communists, whose power had grown during the resistance, and the old political class, which mostly had either fled, been passive or had collaborated with the occupiers. But civil war was not inevitable. The Communist Party in fact joined the newly formed government of George Papandreou, a sign that it could play a role within the country's political institutions. That conciliation was partly due to the moderation and risk-aversion of its leader, George Siantos.[65] Opposition to communism grew, however, and it realigned the country's politics: "the perceived Communist threat made strange bedfellows of Greece's more prominent political personalities."[66] Soon enough the government of national unity collapsed:

The Communists' uneasy coexistence with their adversaries broke down in early December 1944 when Papandreou, frightened by the continuing leftist influence in the countryside, where the resistance organizations remained the dominant force, ordered ELAS [National People's Liberation Army] disarmed and disbanded. In the tense and devious negotiations that followed, the prime minister received the full backing of Britain's embassy and military authorities in Athens. The Communists and their allies in EAM [political wing of ELAS], who now left the government in protest, saw the move to disarm ELAS as an attempt to deprive them of their most potent weapon and to banish them from the political arena.[67]

The refusal to disarm triggered a series of crisis that came to be known as *Dekemvriana*, during which the royalists, aided by the British, defeated the communist forces in Athens. This new power constellation paved the way for the Varkiza Agreement that "provided for the disarming and disbanding of ELAS, the restoration of civil authority, a plebiscite on the issue of the king's return, and national elections for a constituent parliament."[68] But the *Dekemvriana* also eroded public support for the communists, which "moderates [blamed] for the recent violence,"[69] and bolstered support for the monarchy, which was seen as a bastion of stability amidst crisis despite its previous unpopularity. The communists and other leftists abstained from the March 1946 parliamentary elections and the September 1946 referendum on the return of the monarch. Even before the civil war started, therefore, the communists had been marginalized, due to political maneuvering, due to foreign support for the royalists and due to strategic mistakes such as the boycotting of the elections (which the Communist Party in retrospect acknowledged to have been a mistake). The civil war thus started when the communist party was weakest—a reality best understood by two facts: a leadership change which returned Nikos Zahariadis, the movement's natural leader, to power, and by either miscalculation or overpromise of foreign support by the Yugoslavs and, less so, the Soviets.[70] Zahariadis was bolder and more doctrinaire, but the international environment did not favor the communists. The Soviet Union abstained from active interference in the war, following Stalin's pledge to Churchill that Greece would come under the Western sphere of influence after the Second World War; Tito's Yugoslavia pulled its support from the Greek communists when the latter supported Stalin in his battle with Tito; and American support under the Truman Doctrine overwhelmed the communist forces.

The end of the civil war brought relative peace but not normalcy or legitimacy. Fear that left-wing politics could pave the way for communism remained a constant worry of the center, the right, the palace, the military and the US embassy, which replaced the British as the most important foreign player in Athens. From 1949 to 1967, Greek politics were full of intrigue, alliances and counter-alliances, coalitions and counter-coalitions, plotting and counter-plotting—all the result of a country without institutions that allowed for power to be contested and transferred freely.

The persecution of communists and communist-sympathizers continued, and "although a new constitution afforded guarantees of basic political liberties, these were frequently negated in practice by emergency legislation introduced during the civil war [...] A key instrument of political control was the requirement for police clearance for those who sought state employment, a passport or even a driving license."[71] Dissent was still punished: "Actively opposing the right in Greece, even electorally, was an act that could become synonymous at any given moment with imprisonment, exile, torture, or even—in the extreme cases involving members of the communist party following the left's defeat in the Civil War—execution."[72] Perhaps the most visible attack on the left was the killing, in a May 1963, of leftist deputy called Gregory Lambrakis, by "assassins ... drawn from the sinister underworld of the far right, the 'parastate' as it was known, [which] were subsequently found to have links with senior germanderie officials."[73] The rationale for such persecution declined with time:

> Between 1951 and 1961 increasingly vocal demands, not only from the far left, had been made for the liberalization of the repressive apparatus of the anti-communist state that had been established during the civil war and retained during the almost unbroken period of right-wing government since its end. Not only did the communist party remain illegal, but exiled communists continued to be stripped of their Greek nationality. Various forms of discrimination continued to be practiced against known or purported leftists, including the insistence of a 'certificate of social reliability' as a precondition of government employment and even obtaining a driver's license. Although those imprisoned or exiled for their activities during the civil war declined steadily during the 1950s and early '60s from a peak of 20,000, somewhat over 1,000 remained in detention for political offenses.[74]

The military retained an active role in politics, and the threat of a *coup d'état* was forever present in the post-war era. After all, Greece had entered the Second World War with a military government. In 1951, retired General Nikolaos Plastiras boasted to the US ambassador that, "I've kicked two kings out, and if at any point you want the present one to go, just let me know."[75] In the September 1953 elections, the two main political partied were both headed by retired military men—one was Plastiras and the other was Marshal Alexandros Papagos, who had just resigned from the army following a disagreement with the palace and who was "the

victor of the Albanian campaign in the autumn of 1940, the
commander-in-chief during the latter stages of the civil war
and a man of undoubted prestige."[76] Papagos personally
intervened to stop a coup on May 31, 1951, after he resigned from active service, evidence of continued agitation
in the armed forces.[77] (Papagos ruled Greece from November 1952 through his death in October 1955.) In the 1961
elections, George Papandreou "charged that the Greek military, acting on orders from its chief of staff, General Vassi-
lios Kardamakis, 'bent every effort to deliver a heavy vote
for [K]aramanlis'."[78] These elections were tainted with alle-
gations of fraud (which observers discounted), and they undermined whatever stability the country had found after
eight years of uninterrupted right rule. Just two years later,
Kardamakis expressed to the US attaché "concern that Karamanlis would be ousted and sought US support for a
coup," which he did not get.[79]

Leading up to the 1967 coup that finally installed a military government, most political players acted and reacted
based on how they calculated the odds of a coup. Andreas
Papandreou, who was more popular and more powerful,
and whose rhetoric and radicalism produced the anxiety that
the coup plotters used to justify their action, "ridiculed the
idea of a military coup. Margaret Papandreou [his wife], re-
called that, despite ample warnings from US officials, her
husband and their lieutenants were convinced that the king
controlled the army and that, in any case, the United States
would prevent a coup."[80] The military was no monolith, of
course. The 1967 coup was organized by mid-level officers
(hence its name as the Colonels' junta), without the know-
ledge of their superiors, and twice during the Colonels' rule
(in December 1967 and in May 1973), units mutinied and
launched a counter-coup. Opposition to the junta kept
growing, and the military regime finally collapsed after a
failed effort to unite with Cyprus triggered a Turkish invasion in the island.

The other center of political gravity was the Palace (from April 1947, Greece had two kings, Paul and Constantine II). The royal family intervened frequently in the affairs of the state, both to ensure its own stature in politics and to prevent politicians it did not like from gaining power. During the civil war, the king "frequently suggested installing Marshal Alexander Papagos ... as prime minister that would answer to the Palace and not parliament."[81] In period 1950—1952, the Palace "[undermined] the broadly based coalition government of Alexander Diomedes," and did its best to limit the influence of Plastiras after the 1950 elections.[82] When Plastiras formed a government, "the royal couple assured US officials that they backed the new cabinet while at the same time they began undermining their new prime minister."[83] The Palace then tried to bring Papagos from active service into politics to counter the influence of Plastiras, then reversed course, which led to a rift with Papagos.[84] Queen Frederica, a powerful and visible personality, caused tensions with the US embassy, prompting Papagos, by then prime minster, to once "[launch] into a diatribe against the palace."[85] In July 1954, the king "told the newly arrived US ambassador Cavendish Cannon that he favored immediate elections," despite the fact that elections were last held less than two years prior and the government remained popular.[86] When Papagos died, the Palace turned to Constantine Karamanlis to form a government, a junior minister, who was seen, however, as a reliable monarchist. Then, in 1963, Karamanlis resigned as prime minister because of a public clash with the royal family, when the latter decided to take a trip to London against the prime minister's advice (he thought the protests they would encounter would be counter-productive). After Karamanlis went into self-imposed exile, the Palace clashed with George Papandreou over the latter's plan to reorganize the top echelons of the military—and the king repeatedly refused to hold elections that would have benefited Papandreou. In all,

The royal family was largely out of touch with the needs of their subjects and as absorbed in their own self-preserving maneuvers as the much-criticized politicians. The conservative and snobbish social views and ostentatious lifestyle of the royal couple were out of step with the views of an egalitarian and relatively poor Greek society. The monarchs generally acted more as leaders of the 'political royalists" than as a unifying force above politics. In fact, the king and queen thrived on the political instability that allowed them to manipulate public policy.[87]

The third center of political gravity was the United States. Starting with the Truman Doctrine (1947), which pledged aid to the Greek government during its civil war, and continuing with the Marshall Plan (1948—1952), which pumped hundreds of millions of dollars into the Greek economy, the United States became the paramount foreign partner in the country. In the 1950s, the Americans were mostly guilty of statements that triggered accusations of "interference" in Greece's internal affairs. After the 1950 election, the US ambassador threatened that "continued instability and talk of fresh elections might jeopardize American aid,"[88] and when Sophocles Venizelos resigned from office soon thereafter, he "[proclaimed] himself the innocent victim of US intervention."[89] Van Fleet, who had served as the military chief for the US mission, accused Plastiras of being a "communist" in a *New York Times* interview, partly in response to a request from the Palace.[90] Most glaringly, the US ambassador stated a public position on which system Greece should hold elections under, a still contentious issue in a country where each government tried to manipulate the electoral law to suit its interests. By 1959, the Central Intelligence Agency (CIA) became more actively involved and "undertook a major covert-funding operation in Greece,"[91] aimed at weakening support for popular candidates of the

United Democratic Left (EDA). What most hurt the United States and its reputation in Greece, however, was its perceived role in the military coup and junta that ruled Greece from 1967 to 1974. The embassy was surprised by the coup, although its role at the time was seen as much stronger; Andreas Papandreou noted that, "The colonels supported both by the Pentagon and the CIA beat the generals and the king to the punch on April 21, 1967, through the forceful seizure of power and the establishment of a military dictatorship."[92] After a counter-coup failed in December 1967, and the king fled the country, the Americans came to believe that there were no "practical alternatives" to the junta.[93] Over time, and especially after the Nixon Administration took power in Washington, the Americans made their peace with the colonels. In September 1970, the Americans lifted an arms embargo on the junta, and the junta benefited from high level visits from American officials, including Commerce Secretary Maurice Stans, Vice President Spiro Agnew, and Secretary of State William Rogers. In retrospect, the American factor was put at the center of the Greek historical narrative: "The United States served as a national piñata, trooped out by left and right, on every possible occasion, to assuage feelings of humiliation and to avoid a national debate over the real causes of both the rise of the Colonels and the Cyprus disaster."[94]

The 1980s—Populism and Economic Decline

The political system was thus unable to cater to the growing expectations that prosperity had created in the Greek public. At worst, the state was repressive, sent its opponents into exile, tortured them or killed them. At best, it was pulled on so many directions by so many competing forces that it was often paralyzed as a result. This was the backdrop for the electoral success, in October 1981, of Andreas Papandreou's PASOK party. His message rested on defending the "non-privileged," a term that was both loose and inclusive, and on anti-Americanism, acting as a lightning rod for most of what went wrong in Greece. As prime minster, Papandreou reshaped the country's politics, economy and society; he was eloquent, fierce and flexible:

> At any moment, over any given issue, Andreas Papandreou became whatever he claimed himself to be: prime minster, party leader, head of a popular movement, revolutionary agitator, scourge of the Americans, faithful NATO ally, anti-European, grand European, jingoistic and rabid anti-Turk, Balkan federalist, megaloideatis [irredentist], Marxist internationalist, defender of the working class, last best hope of the shipowning caste, man of the people, Spartacus, Pericles, Don Juan.[95]

PASOK's contribution was to allow Greeks "to be progressive and belong to the Left without bearing the stigma of communism."[96] That is why one analyst quipped that "if PASOK had not been created by Andreas Papandreou, it should have been invented."[97] But opportunism mattered more than ideology, and political survival was a greater motivating force than any one agenda. And there is no better way to enhance one's political survival by spending money—lots of money. The chief political contribution of 1980s PASOK, wrote Peter Pappas, was "to take the old clientelistic structure of control and reward and 'massify' it."[98] Increased state spending on wages, pensions, and other transfers, heighted interference in the economy, extended regulation, electoral tax evasion—these were all features that PASOK bestowed to Greek politics after eight years in power.

The result was a wrecked economy. Here is how the OECD described Greece in 1991: "Greece has entered the 1990s facing what are probably the largest imbalances of all OECD countries ... Macroeconomic performance, highlighted by a general government deficit of nearly 20 per cent of GDP, inflation at around 20 per cent and a current external deficit of 5.5 per cent of GDP ($3.6 billion), is practically the worst in the OECD area."[99] Economic indicators reveal a grim picture. Living standards stagnated from 1980 to 1993. Industrial production grew by just 0.4% a year, while investment declined by 1% a year. Rampant inflation meant prices in 1993 were nine times higher than in 1980. The relative importance of trade peaked in 1981 and then fell through 1994. Unemployment kept rising and did not stabilize or start falling until the mid-2000s. Public debt rose to 99% of GDP in 1993. Per capita incomes were 26% lower than the EU-15. The gap had widened again, and the economic miracle was over. How did that happen?

Put simply, the state happened. The 1980s brought an unprecedented expansion in state spending and interference in the economy, derailing both public finances and economic activity. The economy changed in several ways.

Increased state spending. The prosperity of the 1950s—1970s had left Greece with a sizeable but not omnipresent state. But government spending then rose from 30% of GDP in 1980 to 45% in 1990, a 50% hike. Revenues grew only by a sixth, however, meaning that the boost in spending was financed chiefly by public borrowing. Government debt rose fifty percentage points from 22% of GDP in 1980 to 72% in 1990. Higher spending came from more and higher wages for civil servants, price controls for state-owned enterprises that created a need for budgetary infusions, more social transfers, chiefly for pensions, and higher spending to service the country's increasingly sizeable debt.

More civil servants. "Between 1981 and 1990, public sector employment increased at an average annual rate of about 4 percent—around four times as fast as in the private sector." From just over 500 thousand in 1981, the civil service reached almost 700 thousand in 1989.[100] Data before 1980 is scant, however, and a 1988 survey on public sector employment noted that the government had last compiled comprehensive statistics for 1963 (which put employment at

115 thousand).[101] Even so, the government's wage bill rose from eight to twelve percent of GDP in 1980—1990.[102] More people did not mean more or better services. Quality fell as hiring reflected the need of politicians to buy votes rather than a genuine need to provide services. Especially harmful was a 1983 law that "crippled government machinery. It abolished the hierarchy and sapped co-ordination between divisions, even within the same ministry, undermined the authority of senior and competent personnel and made the administration even more liable to political pressure than before."[103]

Subsidies for state-owned enterprises. The role of public enterprises changed in the 1980s. Serving the public by providing goods and services became secondary to meeting social and political purposes by offering an additional outlet for patronage through public employment (besides the civil service) and by "implementing broader policy objectives unrelated to their primary objective of providing goods and services."[104] Between 1980 and 1985, employment at public enterprises rose by a quarter.[105] The 100—150 thousand people who worked there enjoyed generous compensation and benefits, 85% above the average compensation in the private sector in 1997 and 100% higher in 2008.[106] Public enterprises also cost the treasury:

- Intercity Rail: In 1990, OSE, the railroad company, raised enough revenue to cover 32% of its costs (excluding pension obligations), versus 57% in 1980. Between 1980 and 1985, the number of employees rose by a quarter, although it later declined—in 1990 it was 10% above 1980. However, the labor force became more permanent—from nine in ten in 1980, almost all employees (98%) were permanent in 1990, an effective 20% increase in permanent staff during the decade. But passenger-kilometers grew by only 2.3% during the entire decade, and the transportation of merchandise increased by even less, 1.8%. OSE transported about as much in 1990 as in 1980 but its staff increased, it became more permanent, and the company did not raise prices to cover its costs.[107]

- Postal services. Revenues covered 84% of expenses in 1980 and by 1990, they covered 76%. The number of employees rose by a third from 8,883 to 11,899 in that time, and in just one year (1981), the post office opened 464 offices, a 54% increase relative to the 880 it had in 1980. It then started to close these offices, ending the decade with 930.[108]

- Transportation (urban and interurban): Receipts from urban transport in Athens (rail and road) rose three-fold in 1980—1990, but since the price level increased by six times, real revenue shrank by almost half. This real price decrease did little to stimulate demand, however: the number of passengers traveled grew by less than 5% in total from 1980 and 1990, while the number of private cars in Athens doubled.[109] Road transportation more broadly showed a similar trajectory: due to inflation, real revenues went down by 40% during the 1980s.[110]

- Telecommunications. OTE, the national telecom company, was an exception. Its staff actually shrank by 7% in the 1990s, and from losses in 1980, it reported profits of 41 billion drachmas in 1990, against total revenues of 222 billion, an 18.5% margin.[111]

Public enterprises were thus almost uniformly worse off in 1990 than 1980, although many were unprofitable to begin with. The cumulative effect on the economy was sizeable: "From 1984 to 1997, the annual gross financing needs of the nearly 50 public enterprises have averaged about 4 per cent of GDP per year, and current and capital transfers from the state budget averaged about 2 per cent of GDP annually."[112] More generally:

> The cost [of public enterprises] to the economy consists
> not only of an annual drain on the budget of about
> 3.5% of GDP, but a sizeable brake on activity as the
> economy is often deprived of essential inputs at low
> cost. To a large extent, budget transfers to public enter-
> prises are financed by EU funds but they nevertheless
> represent a diversion of these funds from other uses. If
> accumulated over the past decade and half [1982-1997],
> and added to other government liabilities due to public
> enterprises, they represent a burden equivalent to about
> 50% of GDP.[113]

More social transfers. Spending on social transfers as a
share of GDP rose by two-thirds in the 1980s from less
than five percent of GDP to over nine.[114] Pensions accounted for three-fourths of that increase. In August 1981, a
law expanded coverage to the elderly who had not made
contributions, thus boosting the number of people receiving
pensions from social security organizations by a fifth.[115] Social spending on old age insurance as a share of GDP rose
by a quarter from 1981 to 1982.[116] Increased spending
changed Greece's relative position among the OECD—
from ten percent below average in 1980, public spending on
pensions was almost sixty percent higher than in other
OECD countries. Only Germany spent marginally more on
old age than Greece did in 1990.[117] The growth in spending,
however, was unmatched by a growth in contributions. The
social security funds turned from surplus to deficit. In 1980,
subsidies made up six percent of the contributions to the
various social security funds—by 1990, it was almost twenty
percent.[118] Besides spending on old age, there was an increase in family-related spending and on invalidity pensions
which "were often used to replace old age pensions when
the eligibility criterion for the latter could not be ful-

filled."[119] The number of people claiming an invalidity pension rose by two-thirds in the 1980s.[120] Besides boosting spending without a corresponding increase in revenues, subsidies and grants to social security funds "represented a large diffusion of fiscal authority to many and heterogeneous 'parastate' centers of decision-making."[121] The impact of increased social spending thus transcended arithmetic and affected the state's capacity to control and rein in spending.

Higher spending to service debt. Between 1980 and 1994, the cost of servicing debt rose nine-fold. By 1994, the state spent more to service debt than on pensions. Partly, Greece had a lot of debt and so it paid more to service it. But the state's call on funds also pushed up borrowing costs as the banking system struggled to keep up. In 1980, fifteen percent of bank lending went to the state; by 1990, it was a quarter.[122] Interest rates rose despite regulations to keep them low.[123] The growth in interest rates also complicated corporate finance: "The higher cost of credit has weighed heavily on the profits and investment of non-financial enterprises, the latter having accumulated substantial debts. Partly reflecting the substantial debt of ailing firms, the debt/equity ratio for Greek industry is three, which is the highest figure for any of the OECD countries for which statistics are available."[124]

Tax evasion. Since spending rose faster than revenues, tax evasion, a chronic problem, began to get more attention.[125] Until 1978, for example, the word rarely showed up in the OECD's *Economic Survey of Greece*. But the 1979 survey mentioned it as many times as all the previous twelve surveys combined. After a lull, it got ~13 mentions per survey from 1986 to 1996. In the past, tax evasion was an opportunity cost—if the state had more money, it would have made more investments. But given deteriorating finances, lower revenues meant wider deficits, more debt and higher interest rates. It was also in the 1980s that tax evasion became more political. In 1985 and 1989, both election years, revenues as a share of GDP dropped by half a percentage point, halting an otherwise steady increase. As two analysts noted in the late 1980s, "This is clear evidence of laxity in tax enforcement and/or conscious lags in tax collection during an election year."[126] These changes had profound political and economic implications:

> Tax evasion as a broad social phenomenon is coterminous with the syndrome of planning and engaging in unreported and recorded economic activities. When these activities reach a massive scale, they permeate social mores and make tax reform all the more inconceivable in political terms. In PASOK's case, moreover, the dearth of tax revenues led increasingly to public domestic borrowing in the 1980s. The billions or trillions of drachmas that thus escaped taxation effectively became a pool of loan capital provided to the state at interest.[127]

Table 3—Greece: Effective Tax Burden by Source of Primary Declared Income
tax paid as percent of declared income

Year	Total	Rentiers	Merchants	Farmers	Salaried workers	Self-employed	Pensioners
1975	6.0	10.2	7.8	3.7	3.6	10.2	5.2
1976	6.6	10.1	7.8	4.1	4.7	11.3	6.5
1977	7.8	10.6	8.8	6.2	6.1	13.1	7.7
1978	7.8	10.7	8.5	5.9	6.1	13.5	8.3
1979	8.9	12.1	11.5	9.3	6.4	15.1	8.4
1980	10.4	13.2	12.2	9.8	8.2	17.3	10.6
1981	9.2	12.1	11.0	6.2	7.1	16.1	9.8
1982	10.0	12.1	11.4	8.3	8.2	16.0	11.1
1983	10.9	12.3	14.8	6.7	8.9	15.1	10.8
1984	9.7	11.6	11.1	6.0	8.7	14.4	9.1
1985	11.5	12.7	12.4	6.9	10.2	16.3	12.6
1986	10.3	11.3	11.6	5.7	9.1	15.2	10.7
1987	11.2	12.0	14.0	7.3	9.3	17.2	11.2
1988	11.0	13.1	14.4	8.3	8.6	17.2	11.1
1989	8.5	10.1	11.3	3.4	6.6	13.7	8.8
1990	8.6	9.9	11.4	3.1	7.0	14.6	8.0
Δ: '80-'90	-1.8	-3.3	-0.7	-6.7	-1.2	-2.7	-2.6

Source: Based on data from ELSTAT, Public Finance Statistics

Tax evasion transcended a mere weakness in tax collection, however; it included also, a gradual erosion of the tax base. One measure of this change is the effective tax rate, calculated as the ratio between taxes paid and declared income. In 1975, taxes paid accounted for six percent of total declared income. Over time, this ratio rose to 10.4% in 1980 and even 11.5% in 1985, at which point it started to fall. It experienced an even sharper decline in 1989—1990, at 8.5—8.6%. There is too much variation to offer a simple comparison between 1980 and 1990, but there is a decline across almost all income groups. In particular, the tax burden on farmers dropped precipitously. In 1990, they accounted for a mere 0.75% of total declared income but they paid an even smaller share (0.27%) of the tax. More generally, farmers saw a reversal in their relative position in the 1980s:

> In line with EEC farm price policies, but also due to growing net EEC transfers to agriculture from 1981 onwards, the latter's share in national income reached nearly 20 per cent in 1984, the highest ratio over the last fifteen years. In addition, since a sizeable part of growing government transfers have been channeled to farmers, and farmers pay virtually no income tax and social security contributions, the growth in real after-tax income has been considerable since the end of the 1970s, both in absolute terms and relative to that of employees.[128]

It is no wonder that the share of total returns which claimed farming income as their primary source rose from 0.65% of the total in 1980 to 1.92% in 1990 (it was 7% in 2010).

More state intervention. Greece had never been a *laissez faire* economy; MacVeagh, a US ambassador, had "described prewar Greece as 'a country operating almost completely under the principles of a planned economy'."[129] But intervention grew in the 1980s. A new wage-setting system, the automatic indexation adjustment (ATA), passed in 1982, created an inflationary spiral and weakened the link between wages and productivity: "Basic wages in the public and quasi-public sectors (including banks) were raised every four months, on the basis of past inflation up to 1986 and according to officially projected inflation ever since ... During most of the 1980s, ATA was virtually compulsory in the private sector and wage-earners usually looked upon ATA increases as a minimum."[130]

The state also intervened to control prices and profits and to preserve jobs: "In order to prevent dismissals, especially in the absence of other industrial employment opportunities in the same region, governments have opposed plant closures and lay-offs by individual firms. Administrative procedures, political leverage and the desire to avoid social friction have rendered redundancies difficult, even in declining industries."[131] The structure of bank financing further complicated rationalization: "The traditional policy of shoring-up ailing industries has been strengthened by the close links between banks and firms, which may take the form of significant equity holdings and participation in management. These ties make it difficult for banks to withdraw their financial support from loss-making firms."[132]

Shrinking industry. Increased state control squeezed profits which turned negative in 1982.[133] Investment halved between 1973 and 1987 (from 43% of GDP to 21%): "Greece invested one-fifth less than the OECD average and a third less than Spain or Portugal in the 1980s."[134] Industrialization too came to an end. The share of industry in GDP had risen from 25% in 1960 to a high of 32% in 1973 before reaching ~30% in 1980. By 1989, this share had fallen to its mid 1960s levels and in 1994, industry accounted for a smaller share of value added than in 1960. Services become more and more important.

Less, and different, trade. The importance of shipping declined: from peak (1981) to trough (1986), receipts from shipping fell by 45%, and they did not surpass their (nominal) peak until 1992, remaining steadily below tourism and remittances. In part, this was due to weak global demand for shipping as a whole. But Greece also lost its relative position: Greek ship-owners were hit hard in the 1980s, and by 1989, their fleet had halved and so had their global market share from twelve to six percent.[135] Tourism also fell by a third from peak (1981) to trough (1983), but then recovered quickly. By 1989, however, receipts from tourism exceeded their 1981 peak by a mere five percent in dollar terms, even though the number of arrivals into Greece had grown by half. The sharp and steady devaluations of the drachma meant dollar receipts per tourist fell by a third.[136] Remittances, which had declined by a third in 1979—1985, started to boom again, reached an all-time peak in 1987 and overtook shipping in 1990. Greece also started to receive transfers from the European Economic Community (EEC). In 1985, EEC transfers surpassed remittances, in 1986 they surpassed shipping, and in 1989 they surpassed shipping as the most important item in the invisibles part of foreign trade. Here is how the contribution of each item to the invisibles balance changed from 1979—1981 to 1988—1990 (totals across three years to lower volatility):

Shipping from 28.2 to 13.5 percent
Remittances from 17.8 to 14.4
Tourism from 28.8 to 20.8
EEC transfers from 0.8 to 22.3
Other from 24.4 to 29.1.

The 1980s reshaped Greek trade—and even though the drachma fell almost fourfold against the dollar, exports as a share of GDP kept declining.

▪ ▪

The 1980s changed Greece. The state expanded by hiring
more people and by spending lavishly on pensions and social transfers, including state-owned companies. Public finances were in disarray. Debt had risen to alarming levels
and, and the state spent more on debt service than on
pensions. The pull on credit increased borrowing costs,
hurting private industry. Onerous controls and interventions
weakened the private sector. The post-war industrialization
trajectory halted, investment and productivity stagnated.
Transfers from Europe become more important than traditional exports. Greece's convergence with Europe was over.

Incomes were unlinked to effort for more and more
people: "Large sectors of the population ... through government transfer and consumption, have managed to increase substantially their standard of living without a corresponding greater work effort."[137] Or, more generally:

> One worrying aspect is the extent to which Greek soci-
> ety exhibits features typical of a "rentier" mentality.
> Sizeable foreign-exchange inflows from Greeks living
> abroad, the recent large EEC payments and fast-
> growing government transfers to households, have ap-
> parently created a climate of complacency, dissociating
> income from work effort, reducing work incentives and
> favouring consumption. Up to mid-1985, development
> needs of the economy would seem to have been subor-
> dinated to the aspirations of the population for continu-
> ing rapid increases in living standards at the expense of
> capital accumulation and external equilibrium.[138]

The economy was bifurcated. A parallel system emerged
to meet needs that the state did not provide: "In some sectors public and private systems are not complementary, but
superimposed, so that there is duplication involving a waste
of resources at the national level. To a great extent these
systems have developed because of the malfunctioning of

the public sector."[139] Private schools, private clinics and doctors and private cars rose to compensate for faltering public services. Profitability too was divided: "Greek manufacturing industry is composed of two distinct sub-groups—dynamic private firms, with very high profit rates, and ailing (mainly state-controlled) firms, cumulating losses year after year."[140] In the 1980s, half to three-quarters of the country's 3,000+ firms were profitable and their return on equity averaged 20%.[141] The division between public and private became more important than the division between urban and rural.

In the late 1980s, Greece's political economy had changed. There were a growing number of people for whom effort and reward were disconnected, either because accountability was low or because wage-setting systems guaranteed pay hikes. There was a growing dissatisfaction with public administration from civil servants who saw their jobs become politicized and from citizens who could no longer access quality services. There was a growing rigidity in the political system as patronage, subsidies, payments and regulated built a constituency against reforms. And there was a growing middle to upper class that sought services outside the public sector, enjoyed high returns on equity, often courtesy of protective regulations, and continued to pay low taxes.

Recovery, Convergence and the Eurozone

The economy needed help. Here is how the OECD diagnosed the situation in 1992:

> When the New Democracy party formed a new government after the April 1990 elections, the economy seemed to be getting out of control, with inflation running at 23 per cent and the current external deficit and the PSBR (public sector borrowing requirement) at annual rates of nearly 7 per cent and 22 per cent of GDP

respectively, while output began to decline reflecting falling confidence. Moreover, foreign creditors, who financed the meagre growth of the economy during the
1980s, appeared hesitant to continue providing external
finance to support a consumption-oriented economy.[142]

Turning Greece around rested on several initiatives.

Macroeconomic stability. Reducing the budget deficit was
the most urgent task and it came from higher taxes. The
state did not shrink—it was just financed better. Government revenue as a share of GDP rose from 31% in 1990 to
over 43% in 2000, a 12-percentage point jump.[143] Tighter
monetary policy lowered inflation from over 20% in 1990 to
less than 3% in 1999. Granting independence to the Bank of
Greece in 1997 further anchored low inflation. Interest rates
came down, and debt service costs fell by 40%. By 1996,
bank lending to the private sector had been restored to its
1980 level (85% of total credit0.[144] Less money spent on
debt service freed the government to boost other spending.
After a modest decline from 1990 to 1994, primary spending
(excluding debt service) in 1998 was higher than in 1990.[145]

Liberalization. The government "[phased] out of the public sector's privileged access to bank loans and the complete
reliance on financial markets for financing the budget deficit
as from 1994 [and removed] controls on medium and long-
term capital movements in March 1993."[146] And:

> The abolition of the wage-price indexation system, the
> end of government interference in wage bargaining in
> the private sector, deregulation of part-time and tempo-
> rary employment, as well as the possibility of a fourth
> work-shift, the liberalisation of shopping hours, and the
> lifting of price and profit margin controls, have all con-
> tributed importantly to the better functioning of labour
> and product markets since 1991.[147]

Privatizations. The Greek government set ambitious privatization targets to pay down debt and to fix its public finances. Yet these proved unrealistic and the results disappointed: "The total revenue raised from all privatizations (including banks) is equivalent to about 3.5 per cent of GDP (with the bulk raised in 1998), compared with 20.6 per cent in Portugal, 4.0 per cent in Italy and 4.4 per cent in Spain, respectively, during the period 1990–97."[148] Of the $8.2 billion raised in the 1990s, almost half came from selling stakes in OTE, the telecommunications company, which was, by far, the healthiest state company.[149]

Structural funds. From 1989 to 1993, Greece received 7.2 billion ECUs (the predecessor and equivalent to the euro) from Europe. Directly or through co-financing, they accounted for a sixth of total investment in that period. From 1994–1999, European funding made up 11% of total investment and it contributed indirectly to 23% of total capital formation.[150] By 1996, half the government's public investment was covered by EU funds, up from a tenth in 1989.[151] These funds also helped finance investment by public enterprises, whose economic health was questionable. In the late 1990s, when investment drove growth, European funding was essential.

▪ ▪

The 1990s recovery slowed, but did not reverse, the divergence with Europe. In 1999, Greece's income relative to the EU-15 was at its lowest point since the mid-1960s, and convergence only started after 1999. Even then, it was meager. By 2009, Greece's living standards relative to the EU-15 were at their 1984 level and still below the 1978 peak. But the rebound qualified Greece to join the Eurozone as a founding member, albeit admitted with a delay.

The 2000s brought prosperity as well as imbalances. From 2000 to 2007, real per capita income grew by four percent annually and inflation was just over three percent. Unemployment, which kept rising in the 1990s, peaked in 1999 and started to fall. Yet the country imported more than it exported, and its public finances deteriorated. Revenues, which had restored balance in the 1990s, began to slide. The effort that led Greece to enter the Eurozone was hailed as a success, "mission accomplished." The measures, institutions, and practices that boosted revenues faltered, and the country passed tax reforms. Revenues fell from 43% of GDP in 2000 (an all-time high) to 38.1% in 2004. The budget deficit doubled courtesy of lower taxes and the 2004 Athens Olympics (price tag for the state: €7.2 billion[152]). Revenues recovered modestly through 2007, but spending as a share of GDP rose by a fifth, the largest state expansion since the 1980s. Never before had the state spent more than in 2009, and this spending triggered bigger deficits. The 2009 deficit ended up, after several revisions, at 15.6% of GDP. Debt levels reached all-time highs as well.

Greece first got away with these imbalances. By 2006 and 2007, Greek finances had deteriorated, although unreliable statistics helped to obscure the magnitude of the problem. Even so, Greece's budget deficits in excess of five percent of GDP were known by 2006, yet the market was not reacting. It attached to Greek debt "Eurozone" creditworthiness, and the country's borrowing costs in 2004 and in 2007 were about the same.[153] This was a major departure from history. In 1992, derailed finances led to borrowing costs that were three times higher than Germany.[154] In 2007, Greece's borrowing costs were just 7% higher than Germany's.[155] Greece's interest rates should have risen earlier (before end-2009), forcing a fiscal correction before the deficit had risen to 15.6% of GDP. The question is not why Greece got in trouble in 2009 but, rather, why did it not get in trouble sooner.

■ ■

The roots of the Greek crisis can thus be traced to the economic miracle of the 1950s, 1960s, and 1970s, which while delivering prosperity, offered neither legitimacy nor justice to a large share of the Greek electorate. A masterful politician fed on this injustice and mixed it with a deep anti-Americanism, courtesy of the Greek people associating the United States with a junta and the Turkish invasion of Cyprus. The 1980s brought inclusion but not prosperity—the state spent more money, but this was borrowed money; it also manufactured an illusionary improvement in living standards through regulations and controls. The 1980s were a lost economic decade, but the promise of Greece entering the Eurozone provided a foundation for Greek politicians to raise revenue, liberalize the economy, and stabilize the country's finances. Once in the Eurozone, the effort subsided. Spurred on by low interest rates, first government revenues fell and then spending rose after 2006—in fact, it rose massively during the largest expansion in the state since the early 1980s. While money was plentiful worldwide, no one cared. But then money ceased to be plentiful, and Greece came under attack. Greece needed money to pay for its expenses since the markets would no longer lent to it; but it also needed to unravel an economic and political system that had become so entrenched over a thirty-year period.

GREECE'S OPTIONS—AND EUROPE'S

By early 2010, it was clear that Greece could not rely on markets for its financing needs. The debate that ensued on what Greece ought to do was reminiscent of the exchange in *Alice in Wonderland*, where Alice asked the Cat, "Would you tell me, please, which way I ought to go from here?" To which the Cat replied: "That depends a good deal on where you want to get to." Greece had three choices:

- Default. Greece could repudiate its debt (reneging on principal and/or interest); or it could restructure it so that Greece repaid a fraction of the debt over a longer period.
- Default and devalue. Greece could default and issue a new currency, thus exiting the Eurozone.
- Borrow outside markets. Greece could borrow money from the IMF and from European governments to buy time until it was in a position to borrow from the open market again.

The attractiveness of each option depended on the answer one gave to two questions: Was the Greek crisis an economic or political crisis? And was the crisis a Greek or a European crisis?

The IMF, for example, read this as a crisis that was both Greek and economic. In the May 2010 report authorizing a loan to Greece, the IMF wrote: "Greece is adopting an ambitious comprehensive multi-year adjustment program to lower the fiscal deficit and the debt ratio, reduce domestic

demand in line with capacity, and increase supply and competitiveness so that the economy can step onto a higher
growth path led by investments and exports."[1] Of course,
the IMF was fully aware of the difficulties in the international financial environment. But its tone underscored an
economic reading of the crisis with targets regarding the
deficit and the debt, and with policies to meet those targets.

By contrast, a political reading would have said: "Greece
faces a legitimacy crisis. Politicians spend too much state
money to buy votes. The state is weak and cannot perform
basic functions such as law enforcement or tax collection.
Corruption is endemic and markets are dysfunctional. Constituencies benefit from public largesse and enjoy privileges.
The state is too big and inefficient, the private sector too
regulated and insulated from competition. The result is an
uncompetitive economy with excess debt and runway public
finances."

Both diagnoses would lead to similar policy prescrip-
tions: reduce and upgrade the public sector, lower public
spending, and promote competition. But they would measure success in a different way. The economist would ask:
How can Greece pay down debt and reduce its deficits? The
political scientist would ask: How can Greece create political
momentum favoring a smaller and better state and a more
competitive private sector? Reform and escaping the crisis
were linked, but they were not the same. Consider two ex-
amples. Greece could have had a fire sale, raised a hundred
billion euros by auctioning state property, and eliminated the
odds of default. But such course would have entailed no
political or economic reform. Would the crisis have been
solved? Or consider, on the opposite extreme, the passage
of a low, flat tax on all income. The policy would have
boosted investment and lessened tax evasion through a
simpler tax code—but only in time. The short-term impact
on revenues would have been negative, and the odds of default would have risen. Reform and exit from the crisis were

not the same thing.

But could Greece even save itself? Paul Krugman, a Nobel laureate in economics, argued no. Greece's internal problems are "beside the point," he wrote, and have little to do with "the crisis that is tearing Greece apart." Rather, the "the origins of this disaster lie farther north" with the creation of a "deeply—perhaps fatally—flawed monetary system" and with Europe's inept response.[2] Forget Athens, focus on Brussels and Berlin. Shifting the burden to Europe raised another question: what caused the European crisis? The consensus converged on two possible explanations: either the crisis was due to a "deeply—perhaps fatally—flawed monetary system," as Krugman put it, or it was just another financial crisis that could be combated with conventional crisis management tools.

Framing the debate on "what should Greece do" thus required two separate discussions: what exactly was the problem facing Greece; and how did the Greek crisis affect and was affected by the European crisis?

Debt is a Symptom, Not the Disease

Debt merely epitomized several ailments of the Greek economy. As the crisis intensified, the world, and many Greeks, came to appreciate the depth of Greece's woes, which were profound, chronic, and widespread.

Inefficient civil service. Government employment was near the bottom of the OECD, but Greece ranked closer to the top if the calculation included public corporations.[3] The problem, however, was not the size of the civil service *per se*, but its efficacy—or rather, the gap between cost and efficacy. Greece spent, on average, 12% more on the wages of civil servants than the rest of the Eurozone,[4] and public sector employees earned 38% more than employees in the private sector in 2008.[5] Yet the return on investment was low, in part due to unaccountability. For example, Greece was at the bottom of the OECD for use of performance reviews in human resources decisions.[6] Substandard public services were the result. In 2002, Greece ranked second from last in an EU survey of public satisfaction with healthcare.[7] Out-of-pocket spending on healthcare was twice the OECD average (38% vs. 20% of total healthcare spending) as Greeks bypassed the public system and turned to private providers.[8] Greece's educational system tended to rank near the bottom of the OECD Program for International Student Assessment (PISA), which measures ability in reading, mathematics, and science. Greece ranked fifth for students who go abroad to study at the university level (as a share of population, excluding small countries under 5 million people).[9]

Generous spending on pensions. Continuing a trend from the 1980s, spending on pensions kept rising faster than in other countries. Government spending on old age, at 12.3% of GDP, was the fourth highest in the European Union in 2009 and one of the fastest growing.[10] Greece's old-age dependency (ratio of old to working-age persons) ranked it fifth in the world behind Japan, Italy, Germany and Sweden.[11] However, demographics only explained part of the spending on pensions—for example, Germany's old age dependency was higher than Greece's but Greece spent more on pensions than Germany.

Corruption. In 2009, Transparency International ranked Greece at the bottom of the European table with Bulgaria and Romania. In 71st place, Greece was eight spots below Italy, the next European country, which was tied with Saudi Arabia. The survey estimated that 18% of Greek households had paid a bribe in the last year, more than three times the European average and on par with Pakistan and Nigeria.[12] Friedrich Schneider, an authority on estimating the size of underground economies, put Greece's "shadow" economy at the top of the EU-15 table in 2010.[13] The World Economic Forum ranked Greece's judicial independence 75th in the world (out of 133), bracketed by Turkey and Colombia but at least higher than Italy (93rd).[14] Corruption was partly due to a large state and to over-regulation. As Clive Crook once wrote: "Limited government is not worth buying. Markets keep the spoils of corruption small. Government that intervenes left and right, prohibiting this and licensing that, creating surpluses and shortages—now that kind of government is worth a bit."[15] Corruption grows when normal avenues to enrichment are closed.

Tax Evasion. A study put under-reported income by the self-employed at €28 billion in 2009 against total taxable income of €98 billion: "At the tax rate of 40%, the foregone tax revenues would account for 31% of the budget deficit shortfall in 2009."[16] Greece had the highest share of self-employed persons in Europe, almost double the Eurozone average, making tax collection even harder.[17] In June 2011, the Ministry of Finance said that tax arrears stood at €41.1 billion, higher than the entire budget deficit in 2009 (although, arguably, some arrears should have been written off).[18] In 2010, Greece's finance minister noted, in reference to low tax revenues in 2009 that, "The first thing a government does in an election year is to pull the tax collectors off the streets."[19]

Unreliable statistics. As the economic crisis unfolded, all numbers coming out of Greece were suspect. In 2004, the newly installed government had ordered a "fiscal audit" that resulted in significant revisions of Greek deficit and statistics going back to 1997. The revision showed that Greece's 1999 deficit was just above 3%, meaning the country would not have qualified to enter the Eurozone. In September 2006, Greece reported a large revision in GDP (+25.6% for the base year 2000). In October 2009, Greece made significant revisions to its 2008 and 2009 budget deficits. Several times during 2010, Greek and European authorities revised historical statistics, underscoring the lack of proper procedures and paper trails.[20]

Inhospitable business environment. The 2010 Doing Business Report ranked Greece as the 109th easiest place to do business (out of 183). Greece did particularly poorly in the categories for registering property (107th), starting a business (140th), employing workers (147th), and protecting investors (154th).[21] Greece's stock of foreign direct investment was the lowest in the Eurozone and almost seventy percent below the group average in 2009.[22]

Overregulated private sector. Greece's regulations in energy, transport, and communications were more restrictive than other European countries in every sector except postal services.[23] Barriers to entry and licensing fees stymied competition, and they produced profits in wholesale and retail trade twice as high as in several other OECD countries in 2007—2009.[24] When the government introduced a law to deregulate professions, the European Commission published an "Indicative list of professions covered by the new law," noting that, "This non-exhaustive list refers to professions other than those specifically regulated in the law (i.e., notaries, lawyers, architects/engineers and statutory auditors) and explicitly excluded from the scope of the law." The (non-exhaustive) list included over one hundred and thirty professions such as beautician, baker, butcher, barber, beekeeper, bakery-pastry technician, and broadcast network technician—and those are just the ones that start with "b."[25]

Inflexible employment. Greece had a more restrictive labor market relative to the Eurozone on metrics such as rigidity of employment, rigidity of hours, difficulty of redundancy, difficulty of hiring, and relative labor cost.[26] Part-time employment was about a third of the Eurozone average and among the lowest in Europe in 2009.[27] Labor productivity in Greece was half that of the Eurozone average and only higher than Portugal among the EU-15 in 2009.[28] Yet of the twenty European countries that reported a minimum wage in 2009, Greece ranked seventh highest; when controlling for per capita income, it came fourth.[29]

Lack of competitiveness. Greece topped the Eurozone in private consumption as a share of GDP in 2009 (72.4% vs.

57.5%). It also had the largest external deficit save the two
small island states of Cyprus and Malta.[30] Costas Simitis,
prime minister from 1996 to 2004, noted that, "We buy
more goods and services from abroad either because there
are no equivalents in our country or because those offered
are either inferior in quality or more expensive."[31] Meanwhile, Greece employed three times as many people in agriculture versus the Eurozone average, ranking third after
Romania and Poland.[32] The role of agriculture in the economy was the second highest in the Eurozone (after Slovakia)
and twice the group average. The reliance on industry was
near the bottom and services near the top, illustrating the
relative non-diversification of the economy.[33]

Debt was thus a product a deep ailments in the Greek
economy—and a solution should have addressed not just
debt, but also those underlying ailments.

The Eurozone: An Ill-Conceived Union?

Economists had never been enthusiastic about the Eurozone, and as the crisis intensified, their criticism of the
common currency intensified too. Their argument was
based on the theory of "optimum currency areas," which
says entities should share a currency only if they have: labor
and capital mobility; synchronous business cycles; and can
transfer money from one region to another, preferably
through a fiscal union. Even before the Eurozone was born,
economists said the region fulfilled few of these conditions:

> In applying this theoretical framework to economic and
> monetary union (EMU), most economists have com-
> pared Europe with the United States. They have found
> that the countries of the European Union (EU) vary
> more than the regions of the United States, and that la-
> bor much less mobile within Europe than within the
> United States. Thus economists have overwhelmingly
> concluded that the EU is not an optimal currency area

and that EMU cannot be justified on standard economic grounds.[34]

The attraction of a common currency is convenience—wasting no time and money to exchange currencies, and not having to worry about fluctuating exchange rates when making investments, buying goods or planning vacations. By contrast, too many currencies is a hassle, as John Stuart Mill lamented: "So much of barbarism, however, still remains in the transactions of most civilised nations, that almost all independent countries choose to assert their nationality by having, to their own inconvenience and that of their neighbours, a peculiar currency of their own."[35] Robert Mundell, who pioneered the work on optimal currency areas, added that, "In a hypothetical world in which the number of currencies equaled the number of commodities, the usefulness of money in its roles of unit of account and medium of exchange would disappear, and trade might just as well be conducted in terms of pure barter."[36]

Few Europeans would dispute the economic simplicity of a single currency, but such an arrangement carried costs as well. Surrendering the prerogative to issue national currency means that a country outsources some economic decision-making to another authority (in Europe's case, the European Central Bank). Since monetary policy has political and technical dimensions, the gains of a common currency ought to be weighed against this loss of decision-making.

On the political front, monetary policy has distributional effects within an economy and between an economy and the rest of the world. A central bank that increases the money supply by printing currency or by lowering interest rates transfers wealth from one group to another. High inflation benefits debtors and hurts creditors since higher prices reduce the real value of debt. Exchange rate depreciation similarly favors exporters (whose goods are now cheaper overseas) over importers (who have to pay more to buy the same amount). How will those decisions be made? Central bank independence is meant to insulate the institution from political interference, but a central bank can pursue multiple and often competing aims related to price stability or employment. The ECB's mandate is to pursue price stability because that is what the Germans wanted; but, this was hardly a unanimous position. As Martin Feldstein wrote in the late 1990s:

> In a televised speech just before the 1992 French referendum on the Maastricht Treaty [that established the currency union], then-President Francois Mitterrand assured the French public that, contrary to the explicit language of the treaty, European monetary policy would not be under the direction of European central bankers but would be subject to political oversight that, by implication, would be less concerned with inflation and more concerned with unemployment. Mitterrand's statement was a political forecast; France recognizes that the institutions of the EMU would evolve, and continually presses for some form of political body to exert control over the ECB.[37]

The technical dimensions of monetary policy are no less important. A booming region might need credit restrained, a depressed region expanded. Changes in external demand might call for a higher or a lower exchange rate. An entity that cannot rely on monetary adjustment needs alternative methods of adjustment. The conditionality of optimum currency area theory ("only form a currency union if") emerges from this recognition. How did the Eurozone score?

Labor and capital mobility. Mobility is the ultimate adjustment—people and capital can move from depressed to booming areas, relieving pressure from the depressed and damping pressures in the booming areas. Labor mobility in Europe is lower than in the United States, due to barriers that include language and culture.[38] "There were 48.9 million foreign-born residents in the EU in 2011, 9.7% of the total population."[39] By contrast, in the United States, the foreign-born population was 12.9% in 2010, and the share of people who lived in a different state than the one where they were born was 27%.[40] Thus, "natives" made up 90.3% of each European country while they made up only 58.8% of each US state.

Capital mobility in Europe is greater than labor mobility, as money crosses borders more freely and more steadily than people.[41] The typical measure of capital mobility is the correlation between savings and investment. In an autarkic country, investment can only be financed by domestic savings, and they two should be equal. As countries become more open, the correlation breaks down because countries finance investments not just from their own savings but from those of others.[42] Widening disparities between saving and investment, as measured by the current account, in precisely what happened in the Eurozone: "The dispersion of current account positions among OECD countries has steadily increased since the early 1990s, and current account positions have become increasingly related to countries' income per capita. This trend is visible within the OECD as a whole but is stronger within the European Union, and stronger still within the euro area."[43]

Synchronicity. Economies that move in similar ways are more likely to need similar monetary policies. A simple way to assess synchronicity is to look at the average growth rate among Eurozone countries and its dispersion (standard deviation, range from maximum to minimum). Throughout the 2000s, there were countries that grew rapidly while others grew slowly or not at all. Similarly the range from high to low only grew during the decade, evidence that the gap between the best and worst performer in any given year widened. Of course, business cycle synchronicity can be more complicated due to linkages among economies, but a mere glance at the data suggests that at various points, Eurozone countries were experiencing vastly different levels of economic growth. It would be a challenge to set monetary policy that matched both Ireland's economic needs (5% average growth from 2001 to 2007) as well as Portugal's (1.1% average growth from 2001 to 2007).

Table 4—Real GDP Change in Eurozone countries

Country	Entry Year	1999	2000	2001	2002	2003	2004	2005	2006	2007	2008	2009	2010	2011
Austria	1999	3.5	3.7	0.9	1.7	0.9	2.6	2.4	3.7	3.7	1.4	-3.8	2.1	2.7
Belgium	1999	3.5	3.7	0.8	1.4	0.8	3.3	1.8	2.7	2.9	1.0	-2.8	2.4	1.8
Finland	1999	3.9	5.3	2.3	1.8	2.0	4.1	2.9	4.4	5.3	0.3	-8.5	3.3	2.7
France	1999	3.3	3.7	1.8	0.9	0.9	2.5	1.8	2.5	2.3	-0.1	-3.1	1.7	1.7
Germany	1999	1.9	3.1	1.5	0.0	-0.4	1.2	0.7	3.7	3.3	1.1	-5.1	4.2	3.0
Ireland	1999	11.1	10.7	5.3	5.6	3.9	4.4	5.9	5.4	5.4	-2.1	-5.5	-0.8	1.4
Italy	1999	1.5	3.7	1.9	0.5	0.0	1.7	0.9	2.2	1.7	-1.2	-5.5	1.8	0.4
Luxembourg	1999	8.4	8.4	2.5	4.1	1.7	4.4	5.3	4.9	6.6	-0.7	-4.1	2.9	1.7
Netherlands	1999	4.7	3.9	1.9	0.1	0.3	2.2	2.0	3.4	3.9	1.8	-3.7	1.6	1.0
Portugal	1999	4.1	3.9	2.0	0.8	-0.9	1.6	0.8	1.4	2.4	0.0	-2.9	1.4	-1.7
Spain	1999	4.7	5.0	3.7	2.7	3.1	3.3	3.6	4.1	3.5	0.9	-3.7	-0.3	0.4
Greece	2001			4.2	3.4	5.9	4.4	2.3	5.5	3.5	-0.2	-3.1	-4.9	-7.1
Slovenia	2007									7.0	3.4	-7.8	1.2	0.6
Cyprus	2008										3.6	-1.9	1.3	0.5
Malta	2008										4.0	-2.4	3.4	1.9
Slovakia	2009											-4.9	4.4	3.2
Estonia	2011													8.3
Mean, weighted		2.9	3.8	2.0	0.9	0.7	2.2	1.7	3.2	2.9	0.4	-4.4	2.0	1.4
Mean, unweighted		4.6	5.0	2.4	1.9	1.5	3.0	2.5	3.7	4.0	0.9	-4.3	1.6	1.3
Standard deviation		2.8	2.4	1.3	1.7	2.0	1.2	1.7	1.3	1.6	1.8	1.8	2.2	3.0
Maximum		11.1	10.7	5.3	5.6	5.9	4.4	5.9	5.5	7.0	4.0	-1.9	4.4	8.3
Minimum		1.5	3.1	0.8	0.0	-0.9	1.2	0.7	1.4	1.7	-2.1	-8.5	-4.9	-7.1
Max minus min		9.6	7.6	4.5	5.6	6.8	3.2	5.2	4.1	5.3	6.1	6.6	9.3	15.4

Source: Eurostat, extracted November 7, 2012

Fiscal union. The Eurozone was designed not to be a fiscal union, even though it was understood that a common currency would create pressures for a fiscal union. Helmut Kohl, the German chancellor who helped found the Eurozone, recognized that, "Political union is the essential counterpart to economic and monetary union. Recent history, not only in Germany, teaches us that it is absurd to expect in the long run that you can maintain economic and monetary union without political union."[44] Most analysts agreed: "The more fundamental long-term effect of adopting a single currency would be the creation of a political union, a

European federal state with responsibility for a Europe-wide foreign and security policy as well as for what are now domestic economic and social policies."[45] Or, more simply, "Currency union without political union is an unstable half-way house."[46] But political change would be piecemeal, and, at least in 1992, there was no appetite for centralized supervision of finances, especially among the French: "The point was for [France] to gain some control over Germany's currency, not for Germany to gain control over France's budget."[47]

The link between currency and fiscal union is both political and economic. The political argument is that by deferring monetary policy to a centralized authority, states give up some control. Political union is a way to regain it—strong channels through which an entity can petition for favorable policy boosts legitimacy and limits the odds that a country believes that its fate is determined by forces it can neither control nor influence. Equally true is the belief that currency and fiscal union form a natural progression for an entity such as the European Union—and for a continent keen to keep moving forward, this argument holds particular appeal.[48] But there is a difference between political union and a fiscal union where an entity can raise taxes and spend money. The two are linked, of course. Yet it is possible to have political without fiscal union. Fiscal union without political union is "no taxation without representation," and it fails. Political but not fiscal union is "representation without taxation" and it is how supranational entities like the European Union function.

The economic link between currency and fiscal union reflects the constraints of economic policy. Countries can manage an economy through two sets of tools: monetary and fiscal policy. (A third set of tools, reforms, tends to get shortchanged in this particular argument. More on that below.) Without monetary policy, a state in a currency union can only rely on fiscal policy to stimulate a sagging economy. Yet this logic does not explain why the entity practicing fiscal and monetary policy ought to be the same. Presumably, it is to ensure coordination. But with a given monetary policy, states can still adjust fiscal policy at a more micro level. Fiscal policy is a function of the ability to tax and to borrow money which is affected but not determined by a country's currency. This was not a consensus view. Krugman, for example, wrote:

> Consider … what would be happening to Florida right now [2012], in the aftermath of its huge housing bubble, if the state had to come up with the money for Social Security and Medicare out of its own suddenly reduced revenues. Luckily for Florida, Washington rather than Tallahassee is picking up the tab, which means that Florida is in effect receiving a bailout on a scale no European nation could dream of.[49]

But Eurozone countries were not US states. Their citizens did not pay federal income taxes (as do Floridians), and European states could run steady deficits, in contrast to the United States where almost all states were mandated to balance their budgets (Vermont is an exception). And the Eurozone treaty was designed to prevent states from being responsible for each other's debts.

This mattered little. Markets treated all Eurozone debt as equal. The head of global ratings at *Standard & Poor's* admitted that, "The market was scarcely differentiating between any of the 16 sovereign members of the euro zone."[50] A Moody's analyst relayed a 2001 meeting on Greece where "[Moody's] wanted to upgrade the country on the belief that Greece was now part of the euro zone and that nobody was ever going to default and that everything was safe."[51] In 1992, European sovereign debt was a two-tier affair: there was a core group whose governments borrowed at ±8% a year (Austria, Belgium, France, Germany, Ireland, Luxemburg, and the Netherlands), and there was a periphery which borrowed at ±13% (Finland, Italy, Portugal, and Spain). There was also Greece, in a category by itself, with interest rates around 24%. But with time, the gap evaporated. In 1999, when the common currency was launched, borrowing costs were almost the same, and that convergence lasted through 2007.

The convergence in yields supposedly reflected convergent fundamentals: low inflation, stable exchange rates, shrinking deficits and declining public debt. But there was no convergence. Budget deficits shrunk from an average of 4.4% in 1992 to just 0.4% in 1999 and the standard deviation declined too. But by 2007, the standard deviation was higher than in 1992—the Eurozone's members had more divergent deficits. Debt levels showed a similar variability. In 1992, the average level of public debt was 62% of GDP, but the standard deviation was 35%; by 1999, the average debt level had remained flat, but the standard deviation was marginally lower. In 1999, Luxembourg had a debt-GDP ratio of 6% while Greece, Belgium, and Italy were over 90%. By 2007, when yields had fully converged, the average debt level had come down but the standard deviation was unchanged relative to 1999. Inflation was varied too and since the periphery tended to have higher inflation, the convergence in nominal bond yields meant that the more profligate members had lower real borrowing costs. The market was upside down.

By 2007, almost all Eurozone governments financed their deficits at similar costs (although at different real costs). And yet in 2007, there were five tiers of countries:
- Debt below 60% and budget surpluses (Luxemburg, Finland, and Spain)
- Debt below 60% and balanced budgets (Ireland, Slovenia, and the Netherlands)

Table 5—Eurozone Financial Indicators

Country	Entry	Bond yields, %				Budget Deficit, % of GDP				Public Debt, % of GDP				Inflation, %			
		1992	1999	2007	2011	1992	1999	2007	2011	1992	1999	2007	2011	1992	1999	2007	2011
Austria	1999	7.4	4.7	4.3	3.3	-2.0	-2.3	-0.9	-2.6	56	67	60	72	3.4	0.5	2.2	3.6
Belgium	1999	8.7	4.8	4.3	4.2	-8.1	-0.6	-0.1	-3.7	129	114	84	98	2.2	1.1	1.8	3.5
Finland	1999	12.0	4.7	4.3	3.0	-5.5	1.7	5.3	-0.5	40	46	35	49	2.9	1.3	1.6	3.3
France	1999	8.6	4.6	4.3	3.3	-4.6	-1.8	-2.7	-5.2	40	59	64	86	2.4	0.6	1.6	2.3
Germany	1999	7.8	4.5	4.2	2.6	-2.5	-1.6	0.2	-1.0	42	61	65	81	5.0	0.6	2.3	2.5
Ireland	1999	9.1	4.7	4.3	9.6	-2.9	2.7	0.1	-13.1	91	48	25	108	3.2	2.5	2.9	1.2
Italy	1999	13.3	4.7	4.5	5.4	-10.3	-1.9	-1.6	-3.9	105	113	103	120	5.0	1.7	2.0	2.9
Luxembourg	1999	7.9	4.7	4.7	2.9	-0.2	3.4	3.7	-0.6	5	6	7	18	3.2	1.0	2.7	3.7
Netherlands	1999	8.1	4.6	4.3	3.0	-4.2	0.4	0.2	-4.7	77	61	45	65	3.2	2.0	1.6	2.5
Portugal	1999	13.8	4.8	4.4	10.2	-4.4	-3.1	-3.1	-4.2	50	49	68	108	8.9	2.2	2.4	3.6
Spain	1999	11.7	4.7	4.3	5.4		-1.2	1.9	-8.5	46	62	36	68	7.1	2.2	2.8	3.1
Greece	2001	24.1	6.3	4.5	15.8	-11.0	-3.1	-6.5	-9.1	79	95	107	165	15.9	2.1	3.0	3.1
Slovenia	2007			4.5	5.0			0.0	-6.4		24	23	48		6.1	3.8	2.1
Cyprus	2008			4.5	5.8			3.5	-6.3		59	59	72		1.1	2.2	3.5
Malta	2008			4.7	4.5			-2.4	-2.7		57	62	72		2.3	0.7	2.4
Slovakia	2009			4.5	4.5			-1.8	-4.8		48	30	43		10.4	1.9	4.1
Estonia	2011							2.4	1.0		6	4	6		3.1	6.7	5.1
Mean		9.85	4.68	4.37	5.53	-4.45	-0.40	-0.27	-4.50	61.80	62.42	55.67	75.27	5.20	1.49	2.36	3.08
St. dev.		2.37	0.08	0.10	3.52	2.97	2.15	2.99	3.54	35.19	30.01	30.81	38.45	3.92	0.72	0.65	0.89

Notes: Bond yield (EMU convergence criterion bond yields); budget deficit (net lending, excessive deficit procedure); public debt (general government debt); inflation (harmonized price index). Sources: Eurostat, EMU convergence criterion series - annual data, accessed September 25, 2012; EC, AMECO, 11 May 2012; IMF, World Economic Outlook Database, October 2012 (for 1992 inflation rate.)

- Debt from 60% to 84% and roughly balanced budgets (Austria, Germany, and Belgium)
- Debt just over 60% and wider budget deficits (France and Portugal)
- Debt over 100% and either moderate (Italy) or sizeable deficits (Greece).

Convergence, therefore, made no sense. Even without knowing much about the countries that made up the Eurozone, a look at the most basic public finance statistics would suggest that these countries should have different credit ratings and borrowing costs. There was nothing inherent in the Eurozone that said all yields should converge; as Milton Friedman said in 2001, "Different countries will still pay different rates, depending on their credit quality."[52] But they did not, at least not until late 2008. That's when markets recognized that countries with low debt levels and budget surpluses should borrow more cheaply than countries with high debt levels and budget deficits. Except that this correction came amid a broader risk aversion. After years of having access to easy money, markets were now cautious and risk averse. So rather than a return to pricing risk correctly, markets went berserk. As the governor of the Bank of Ireland put it: "We were lured into a false sense of security. Europe took for granted what everyone thought was the automatic effect of economic stabilizers in the monetary union. The financial markets were too complacent. Lax policy was not punished by markets until it was too late."[53]

Pricing sovereign debt correctly rested at the heart of the problem. Any sovereign debt exercise requires divining such difficult questions like political will and commitment to reform. But the market had one extra problem: Would Germany bail out the indebted countries? Would it demand a haircut (private sector involvement) in exchange for more funds? Bond yields since 2008 reflected both the underlying fiscal position of the debtor country and a reading of European politics that changed daily. Much of the volatility in debt markets after 2008 was the result of international politics, not economic fundamentals.

The Ghost of Argentina

The discussion over what Greece ought to do soon became colored by the view that Greece was "the new Argentina." Mark Weisbrot explained:

> [When] Argentina defaulted on its foreign debt and cut loose from the dollar ... Most economists and the business press predicted that years of disaster would ensue. But the economy shrank for just one more quarter after the devaluation and default; it then grew 63% over the next six years. More than 11 million people, in a nation of 39 million, were pulled out of poverty. Within three years Argentina was back to its pre-recession level of output, despite losing more than twice as much of its gross domestic product as Greece has lost in its current recession [by May 2011].[54]

Whether Argentina a model for Greece hinged on two questions: how similar was Greece in 2010 (when it sought a bailout) versus Argentina in 2001 (when it defaulted)? And, what happened to Argentina after default?

In 1999-2001, Argentina's external balance was considerably better than Greece's external balance in 2008-2010. Argentina was running current account deficits of 3 to 5% of GDP, while Greece's deficits were in double digits.[55] So when Argentina defaulted and its imports contracted, the adjustment was minor. By contrast, a Greek default and exit from the Eurozone would have produced a sharp imbalance between exports and imports, and without enough foreign currency to pay for imports, Greek households and corporations would have been denied basic goods, including fuel and medicine.

Table 6—Comparing Argentine and Greek Economic Crises
percent of GDP, except growth

Comparison Years							
Comparison	Argentina	1997	1998	1999	2000	2001	2002
Years	Greece	2006	2007	2008	2009	2010	2011
Current	Argentina	-4.1	-4.8	-4.2	-3.1	-1.4	9.0
Account	Greece	-11.4	-14.6	-14.9	-11.1	-10.1	-9.8
Government	Argentina	23.2	23.8	24.3	24.6	23.6	23.0
revenue	Greece	39.2	40.8	40.7	38.2	39.7	40.9
Government	Argentina	25.3	25.9	28.5	28.2	29.7	38.9
expenditure	Greece	45.2	47.6	50.6	53.8	50.2	50.0
Budget	Argentina	-2.1	-2.0	-4.1	-3.6	-6.0	-15.9
Balance	Greece	-6.0	-6.8	-9.9	-15.6	-10.5	-9.1
Annual GDP	Argentina	8.1	3.9	-3.4	-0.8	-4.4	-10.9
Growth	Greece	5.5	3.0	-0.2	-3.3	-3.5	-6.9

Source: International Monetary Fund, World Economic Outlook Database, October 2012

Government finances were different too. Government revenues and expenditures in Argentina were ~25% of GDP with deficits of 2—4% until 2000. By contrast, Greece had a much larger state and a much larger fiscal hole: as Greece negotiated a bailout in 2010, its budget deficit was four times higher than what Argentina's deficit was in 2000 (the Greek deficit was estimated at 13.6% when the bailout was signed in May 2010). Without access to capital, the Greek government would have been forced to balance its budget either through confiscatory taxes, excessive reductions in spending, massive inflation, or a combination of all three.

Nor was the currency situation of the two countries the same. Argentina had a fixed exchange rate, while Greece had given up its currency. Economically, the difference is trivial since both countries used a currency they did not control. But from a crisis-management perspective, the two structures differed. Argentina kept its pesos and could adjust easily: all the central bank had to do was to refuse to convert pesos to dollars at the prevailing one-to-one rate (as it did). The transition would be simple. Moreover, Argentina could only defend its fixed exchange rate as long as it had enough dollars to exchange for pesos at the one-to-one rate. Devaluation came when government could no longer support that exchange rate. Greece did not have that problem. People could go en mass to the banks and withdraw their deposits, but they could not cause a currency change by asking for euros by giving drachmas. Greece could defend itself more easily. Membership in the Eurozone also helped Greece mobilize an international coalition to help it. A sudden default and exit from the Eurozone would have forced not just losses on European banks, but unpredictable ripples across the Eurozone. The stakes in Argentina were smaller and conventional, in Greece major and unknowable.

Greece's imbalances were thus greater than Argentina's and its defenses were stronger. What about the aftermath? Argentina benefited from a commodity boom in the 2000s which boosted exports—hardly a replicable international environment in the early 2010s. But Argentina's growth came with costs. Official inflation ranged from 8% to 10%, but it was estimated, unofficially, at two-to-three times the official figure—in itself, this fact casts doubt on how much Argentina's standard of living improved.[56] Argentina did not resolve its propensity to run chronic budget deficits—it just shifted the financing mechanism from borrowing to printing money. Both politics and economics suffered. Argentina was ranked 105 in Transparency International's Corruption Perceptions Index 2010, tied with Algeria, Kazakhstan, Moldova and Senegal.[57] In 2001, it was ranked 57.[58] The Heritage Foundation / Wall Street Journal Economic Freedom index showed a similarly sharp decline in economic freedom over the last ten years—the drop is similar to that experienced by Venezuela and just smaller than Bolivia's.[59] Most of the deterioration was attributable to a decline in property rights, financial and monetary freedom, and an increase in government spending. Argentina's Doing Business rank in 2011 was 124—much worse than Greece's 78,[60] while the country's ranking on the World Economic Forum Global Competitiveness Index declined from 70 in 2006—2007 to 94 in 2012—2013.[61]

These observations do not cover every aspect of the Greece-Argentina comparison, but they do underscore that

Greece had more severe imbalances than Argentina, it could defend itself better, and that default and devaluation did little to improve the Argentina's structural weaknesses—hardly a model to copy.

One Crisis, Four Dimensions

Crafting a European and Greek response to the crisis depended not just on politics and economics but on the admission that Europe confronted not just one crisis but four.

Fiscal crisis. The fiscal crisis had two dimensions: high debt and high deficits. In five Eurozone countries, public debt was 90% of GDP or more at year-end 2011 (Greece, Italy, Ireland Portugal and Belgium). Next among the most indebted countries were France (85.8%) and Germany (81.2%). These seven countries made up 82% of the Euro-zone's public debt.[62] Besides high debt, countries had to borrow more. Of the 17 countries in the Eurozone, only one (Estonia) ran a budget surplus in 2011, although six had primary surpluses (excluding interest payments). A full 11 countries had budget deficits that exceeded the 3% limit set by the Maastricht Treaty. Just to finance their deficits, countries in the Eurozone had to borrow €387 billion in 2011. Adding debt rollover would put their financing needs much, much higher.[63] High debt and high deficits mean that borrowing is more expensive as markets start to doubt that the highly indebted countries have credible plans to pay back their debt. Thus, they demand higher yields to be compensated for the extra risk of lending to them. As borrowing costs rise, fiscal positions deteriorate because the projected burden for servicing debt rises. When borrowing costs keep climbing, countries either default or need a bailout.

Banking crisis. The banking crisis was connected to the fiscal crisis, and the link went both ways. One reason was that countries were liable for bailing out banks: "States are individually responsible for rescuing banks in their jurisdictions. As a consequence, states are highly vulnerable to the cost of banking crises-especially when they are home to banks with significant cross-border activities. In 2010, total bank assets amounted to 45 times government tax receipts in Ireland, and the ratio was very high in several other countries."[64] Banks also held sovereign debt, and they held mostly debt of their own governments.[65] If markets were worried about the ability to governments to repay debt, they were worried about the impact of non-payment on those holding debt. Sovereign default would force banks to raise money to offset the losses in their portfolios. If many banks did so at the same time, as happens during a crisis, sellers would outnumber buyers, and prices would fall. The more prices fell, the more banks needed to sell, triggering a downward spiral. Finally, banks were susceptible to confidence shocks—in particular, they saw withdrawals from individuals and businesses who were worried about their euros turning into drachmas, pesetas, liras or escudos. Exit from the Eurozone of one country would lead to capital flight in others.

Economic crisis. European countries diverged in microeconomics and macroeconomics: "The euro area today consists of a competitive, moderately leveraged North and an uncompetitive, over-indebted South."[66] In its *Global Competitiveness Report 2012/2013*, the World Economic Forum showed that relative competitiveness cuts across a geographical diagonal with high competitiveness indices in Finland, Sweden, Denmark, Latvia, Germany, Austria, Malta, the Netherlands, Belgium, the United Kingdom, and Ireland, and low competitiveness in Portugal, Spain, Italy, Greece, Cyprus, Bulgaria, Romania, Hungary, Czech Republic, Slovakia, Slovenia, Poland, Estonia and Lithuania.[67] The periphery tended to have trade deficits and negative international investment positions (owes more to the world than the world owes to it), and it suffered from ailments such as state meddling, red tape, tax evasion, rigid labor markets, generous welfare and state benefits, and regulations that restrict competition.[68] Chronically low increases in productivity and above-average inflation were the result, and structural reforms were the solution.

Political crisis. The politics of the European Union and the Eurozone have never been easy—although the union is popular, its popularity has never been deep. Voter turnout has fallen in every election for European parliament since 1979, reaching 43% in 2009. The 1992 Maastricht Treaty, which established the Eurozone, failed to pass once in Denmark (until it was modified) and it passed narrowly (51%) in France. By contrast, two failed referendums in France and the Netherlands doomed the Treaty establishing a Constitution for Europe in 2005. European elites routinely discuss the project's "democratic deficit."

The crisis hit governments hard, and no leader could count on political survival. By July 2012, governments had changed at least once in thirteen of the seventeen countries of the Eurozone, and "although the conditions in the individual countries have much to do with their unique domestic politics, ultimately their governments were forced from power because they did not have an effective concept for combating the debt crisis."[69] In countries that received bailouts, funding came with demands for unpopular reforms during bad economic times, falling living standards and rising unemployment. Radicalization and extremism spiked.

In funder countries, crisis management undermined the agreements that formed the Eurozone, and politicians lacked the authority to implement many of the measures being proposed. The Germans had wanted a European central bank that was, "Fiercely independent of governments (unlike in the French tradition) and devoted with Protestant fervor to the one true god of price stability (lest the Weimar nightmare of hyperinflation return)."[70] Debts had to be national, not European. Neither did the French want strict fiscal oversight. A July 2012 online poll by Der Spiegel asked Germans, "Do you agree that Germany must continue fighting to save the euro, even if additional billions are required, or do you think it is almost futile, given the developments of recent months?" More than half (54%) answered, "I think it is almost futile."[71]

Weighing the Options

Europe could pursue four options either independently or in a combination:

- Federalize debts. Convert national into European debts by issuing Eurobonds or, indirectly, by having the ECB purchase the bonds of the periphery.
- Restructure debts. Cut the burden of countries with excess debt. Do it quickly, decisively, and, if possible, voluntarily.
- Shrink the Eurozone. Break apart the currency union, or expel the weak links.
- Offer conditional aid. Let countries borrow from the IMF and other European states by pledging to make deep reforms.

The problem is that each option could solve only some of Europe's problems.

Federalize debts. Overwhelming firepower was one way to resolve the fiscal and banking crises, but not the economic or the political ones. Momentum toward reform depended on continuous external pressure rather than a blanket guarantee. Besides, funder countries would be unlikely to endorse a policy that provided a blank check to the periphery. Resolving the fiscal and banking crises in that way would exacerbate the economic and political crises. As Fred Bergsten noted, "An explicit commitment to unlimited bailouts would represent the ultimate moral hazard. It would relieve the debtor countries of the pressure to sell tough political decisions to their parliaments and publics in order to effectively adjust their economies."[72] Or, as Charles Kindleberger put it, "This is a neat trick: always come to the rescue, in order to prevent needless deflation, but always leave it uncertain whether rescue will arrive in time or at all, so as to instill caution in other speculators, banks, cities, or countries."[73] Federalization boasted simplicity but lacked legitimacy, which is why non-Europeans were keener to suggest it than were Europeans. It carried inherent dangers: governments can accept limited sovereignty in exceptional circumstances, but agreeing to a system that delegated, ad infinitum, power away from national governments could be too much. If this crisis had showed anything, it was that Europeans still felt only partly European and easily fell back into national stereotypes and prejudices.

Table 7—The Merits of Different Options in Resolving European Crises

Option	Fiscal	Banking	Economic	Political
Federalize debts.	Solution as long as markets had faith in Germany.	Solution as long as markets had faith in Germany.	Slower push for reforms in the periphery.	Political backlash in the north—fear of moral hazard.
Restructure debts.	Lower pressure on yields for defaulter; higher risk for others.	Banks that held debt that has lost value would need capital injection.	No direct link to reforms.	Support possible, but less so for official aid.
Shrink the Eurozone.	Short-term pressure on remaining countries.	Considerable uncertainty and downside risk.	Growth through devaluation. But reforms less likely.	Some support for expelling some countries. Downside if euro unraveled.
Offer conditional aid.	No final solution. Continued uncertainty.	No final solution. Continued uncertainty.	Incentive for reforms because countries need to secure additional funds.	Support from funder, opposition from recipient countries. Extreme politics and likely radicalization.

Restructure debts. There was no disagreement that countries with excessive debt might have to default on part of their obligations. Of course, restructuring treated the symptom (excess debt), but not the disease that produced it (weak economic fundamentals). Yet default had an obvious appeal by making the defaulter's remaining debt more sustainable. But restructuring carried three risks. First, once the Eurozone de-stigmatized restructuring, the risk premium on all suspect debt would increase. (In practice, markets were already assaulting the weaker Eurozone members.) Second, restructuring would weaken banks that held debt—in extreme cases, it could force recapitalization. And since recapitalization had to come from the sovereign, it created an inescapable vicious cycle for countries with excess debt and weak banking sectors. And third, there was no understanding, at least when the crisis hit, whether restructuring could be done within the Eurozone or whether a country that defaulted would also be forced out. (When Greece restructured its debt in early 2012 without exiting the Eurozone, that question was answered.)

Economists were almost unanimous that Greece should default. Debt was high, and the country has little chance to repay it. Why go throw good money after bad to delay the inevitable? In March 2012, Greece did restructure its debt, reducing it by €87.7 billion (from €368 billion in December 2011 to €280.3 billion in March 2012).[74] And Greece would likely need another one. In March 2012, when Greece signed a second bailout agreement, the official forecasts put the country's debt at 116% of GDP by 2020—hardly a great position.[75] But what were the arguments for and against restructuring when Greece first got into trouble?

The first argument for default was that Greece was insolvent. As Nouriel Roubini put it, "Greece is not just suffering from a liquidity crisis; it is facing an insolvency crisis too."[76] At the time of the first bailout (May 2010), the IMF forecasted that debt by 2020 might be 120% of GDP (versus an estimated 115% at year-end 2009, later revised to 129%).[77] Such level was likely unsustainable—likely, but not surely. Solvency is tricky. In *This Time is Different*, Carmen Reinhart and Kenneth Rogoff chronicled 36 external default episodes for middle-income countries that took place from 1970 to 2008. More than half of those episodes took place when external debt was below 60% of GDP. In only a sixth of the cases did external debt surpass 100%.[78] By contrast,

Greece's 2010 external debt would hit 101.5%, beyond merely worrisome levels. Regarding public debt, Reinhart and Rogoff showed that the total public debt-to-revenue ratios at the time of default for 89 episodes from 1827 to 2003 ranged from about 2.7 in Africa to 4.5 in Latin America (Europe and Asia being between three and four).[79] Greece's number in 2010 was expected to be 3.2, on par with other European countries at the time of their defaults, but low by Latin American standards where debt ratios had been higher.[80]

Yet these numbers were only instructive. If Greece had been Argentina, it would have defaulted in the early 1990s; if Greece were Japan, it would have another decade before facing any trouble. Greece was neither Argentina nor Japan. Greek debt would be unsustainable if the market thought it was unsustainable. Avoiding default would depend on two factors: market appetite for risk and the momentum for change. According to the May 2010 bailout, Greece would have returned to the markets in early 2012. If markets were euphoric, they would lend to Greece easily; if not, they would not. Their appetite would be determined not by the precise level of debt (130 or 140 or 150% of GDP) but by global credit conditions and Greece's trajectory. Good news—lower tax evasion, increased foreign investment, a smaller state, aggressive tackling of privileged constituencies—would have make it easier for Greece to raise money again. Not that Greece's debt was sustainable, but it was not clearly unsustainable, an important distinction.

The second argument for default was that it would free up money that would otherwise go to service debt. Since 2004, Greece spent much more on interest payments than any other European state, and in 2011, it spent 7% of its GDP on interest versus a Eurozone average of 3%.[81] According to the IMF, from 2012 to 2015, Greece would devote almost 8% of its GDP on interest.[82] Default would free up (some of) those resources to allow for fewer spending cuts, higher pensions and salaries, and lower taxes. Stimulus would dampen the recession.

The third argument for default was that sooner was better than latter. Roubini explained:

> The €110bn bail-out agreed by the European Union and the International Monetary Fund in May only delays the inevitable default and risks making it disorderly when it comes … Certainly, it would be better to use a small amount of public money to tempt creditors into a pre-emptive deal now than waste €110bn of it trying to prevent an unavoidable restructuring later. Such public resources would be better used to help ring-fence other embattled Eurozone economies—such as Spain—whose debt may come under renewed pressure.[83]

Roubini was both right and wrong. Orderly was better than disorderly, but earlier was not always better than later. The May 2010 bailout shifted liabilities from the private to the public sector. In March 2010, the Bank of International Settlements put foreign exposure of banks and other institutions to the Greek public sector at $92.5 billion; by December 2011 (the last quarter before default), this number was $22.7 billion.[84] Foreign banks had been bailed out—Europe and the IMF gave money to Greece, which allowed Greece to repay its debts. Restructuring was orderly with minimal fallout because it took so long to come. But even assuming that sooner is better economically, it may not be so politically. How and when a country defaults matters. Default in 2010 would not be the same as default in 2012: "We defaulted because speculators forced us to default and the Europeans did nothing to help us" is a different narrative that "We were given time and €110 billion and yet we failed to avoid default." These two defaults may be the same on paper, but they differ politically. Greece's faith in Europe would have been shaken. Membership in the Eurozone has been a political, not an economic imperative for Greece—which is why public support for the euro remained high no matter what. An exit would have been seen as abandonment. This crisis of faith would have rivaled the anti-Americanism that spiked in Greece after the Colonels' junta and the 1974 crisis in Cyprus. Greece would have felt betrayed and this betrayal would have reopened deep questions about Greece's role in the world and its links to other states. Abandoning the euro would be nothing like Argentina abandoning convertibility. Its political meaning would have been wider and its repercussions far deeper.

The most concrete argument against default was that, at the time of the first bailout, Greece was running and was expected to keep running a primary budget deficit. Even if Greece paid no money to service debt, its budget balance would be short by €5.6 billion in 2010 and €2.1 billion in 2011 (in reality, the numbers turned out to be €5 billion in 2010 and €2.4 billion in 2011).[85] A default in May 2010 would mean that Greece would have to cut its spending and/or increase revenue by €5.6 billion in 2010 and by €2.1 billion more relative to what it did. In truth, since Greece's recession would have been deeper in the event of default, the gap would have been much greater. Plus, these measures would have to have been implemented instantly rather than gradually since the country would be literally out of money.

The second argument against default was that the Europeans did not want it. The damage to the European banking sector and, perhaps, the Eurozone itself would have led to an even greater recession in Greece. The bigger damage, however, would be political. George Papaconstantinou, Greece's finance minister during the first bailout, noted that no one in Europe wanted to hear about default in early 2010—the option was off the table during negotiations.[86] Default would have been against the wishes of the bigger European partners—imposing big political costs on Greece and damaging the country's reputation.

The third argument against default was that it would have wiped out the Greek banking sector. In Q1 2010, 30% of Greece's debt was held by Greeks; by year-end 2010, that number was 47%. Default would create a big financial hole in whatever institutions held Greek debt—a hole that the state would have to fill. This problem became more apparent as Greece negotiated a haircut in its debt in late 2011 and early 2012. The second bailout agreement, signed in March 2012, included €50 billion to "help banks cope with the impact of the recession and of restructuring of government debt."[87] As the IMF noted:

> Bank solvency has become an acute problem. Banks will no longer be able to delay recognition of losses on their government bond holdings, as the PSI [Private Sector Involvement—the haircut] deal will trigger impairments of about €22 billion, compared to system Tier 1 capital of €23.8 billion in September 2011. Regulatory capital will be wiped out for four banks representing 44% of system assets, while the remaining banks would end up significantly undercapitalized.[88]

The problem of supporting Greek banks underscored the peril of a default: the Greek government might reduce its liabilities (debt) but it would have to assume new liabilities (new borrowing) in order to recapitalize the Greek banks that were impaired by the default. That is precisely the reason why the haircut, announced at first to shave off €100 billion in debt, produced almost no decline in Greek debt: as the IMF reported, Greece's 2012 debt-to-GDP was expected to be 163.2% versus 165.3% in 2011.[89]

Shrink the Eurozone. The case for breaking up the Eurozone followed from the premise that the currency union was not optimum. Monetary policy in the 2000s might have suited Germany, but not Spain and Ireland, which suffered from housing bubbles, or Greece and Portugal, which accumulated trade deficits. If monetary policy at the European level was inappropriate, having control revert back to the state level would be a solution.

Two assumptions underpinned this syllogism: independent monetary policy is better than not, and adjustment is possible through monetary policy. Having control over monetary policy and having good monetary policy are not the same. Monetary policy is often a disaster, leading only to chronic inflation. Central-bankers having control over an economy the way a conductor has control over an orchestra is an idea that the 2000s should have deflated. After all, monetary policy in the United States proved overly expansive in the 2000s, helping to fuel a housing bubble. Milton Friedman noted that, "The history of US monetary policy since the establishment of the Fed has many more periods of poor than of good policy."[90] Friedman believed that the calculus of whether to give up monetary policy thus included "an inevitably political question":

How good is monetary policy in A; in B; and how good is it likely to be? In practice, this is often the most important question. Experience suggests that in a small developing country an independent internal monetary policy is likely to be highly unstable, with occasional episodes of high inflation. There is every reason to believe that the monetary policy of the US, or Germany, now the euro, or Britain, however flawed from the large country's own point of view, will provide much more stability than the small country will produce by itself. This has probably been the major factor that has led countries to consider or to adopt a currency board or dollarization.[91]

The Eurozone formed an oasis of stability for several countries. Greece, Portugal, Italy, and Spain had significantly higher inflation than core European states in the early

1990s. The process of entering the Eurozone had helped bring down inflation, and the ECB, for all its flaws, likely produced a more stable currency than what these countries would have achieved by themselves. Independent would not have meant better, and certainly not in countries with weak institutions and no history of central bank independence. Greece, for example, witnessed a secular decline in inflation as the country began the process to join the euro. Inflation fell from almost twenty percent in the 1980s to less than three percent in 1999. In the 2000s, Greece continued to enjoy low inflation, although it was higher than its Eurozone peers. Exit from the Eurozone could have easily left the country with double-digit inflation, just as Argentina experienced after 2001.

Currency union offered stability over flexibility. Slow-growing countries could not lower interests to stimulate their economies nor could they depreciate their currencies to boost exports. Crisis management relied on fewer tools, which was problematic because exports had played a central role in past fiscal consolidations. As the IMF wrote, "A fall in the value of the currency plays a key role in softening the impact of fiscal consolidation on output through the impact on net exports. Without this increase in net exports, the output cost of fiscal consolidation would be roughly twice as large, with output falling by 1% instead of 0.5%."[92] The inability to devalue was the paramount fact in the Eurozone crisis for many analysts. Greek labor costs had grown twice as fast as the rest of the Eurozone from 2000 to 2008.[93] No country experienced a wider gap, and larger trade deficits were the result of an inability to compete. Devaluation would be an instant solution.

But devaluation is no free lunch. In the 1980s, the Greek drachma depreciated sharply against the dollar, and in 1989 a dollar could buy three times as many drachmas as in 1981.[94] Yet such devaluation did nothing for exports, whose contribution to the economy shrank by a quarter. Devaluation as a competitive strategy had several problems. Price is just one way to compete and it is generally the worst. There is no such thing as an expensive product, after all—there is only a product that costs too much relative to what you get. When there is a mismatch between the price and the offering, there are two solutions: change the price or change the offering. Businesses know that lowering the price is only a short-term fix far. Competing on price through devaluation is not the same as maintaining a cost advantage—the former is chiefly an engineering trick, the latter is a spelled out strategy which says "I can do this more cheaply than the competition." The former is an illusion, the latter a business proposition. The former is lazy, the latter efficient. Plus, once price becomes the source of advantage, it can stigmatize a brand. Being branded as a "cheap destination," for example, can be problematic, and Greek tourism suffered in the 2000s from such a fate. That is why, from 2005 to 2011, tourism receipts remained flat despite a 14% increase in arrivals—tourists merely spent less by staying fewer nights. As Simon Anholt, an expert on national reputation, said: "Compare the way consumers in Europe or America will willingly pay more for an unknown 'Japanese' product than for an identical 'Korean' product that is probably made in the same Chinese factory."[95] Brand matters and competing by being cheapest can have long-term negative consequences.

The obsession with devaluation and export-led growth presumed that there was no other way to grow. Yet that assumption was incorrect, as Peter Bauer showed decades ago. His target was foreign aid, but his logic applied to foreign investment and to exports. In his essay *From Subsistence to Exchange*, he wrote:

> To have money is the result of economic achievement, not its precondition. That this is so is plain from the very existence of developed countries, all of which orig-

inally must have been underdeveloped and yet progressed without external donations. The world was not
created in two parts, one with ready-made infrastructure
and stock of capital, and the other without such facili-
ties. ... Indeed, if the notion of the vicious circle of poverty were valid, mankind would still be living in the
Old Stone Age.[96]

Greece had plenty of slack, courtesy of rigid labor markets and red tape. Businesses were not being created, products not being launched, and services not being offered due
to insurmountable barriers. It rarely paid to try big things.
Reform could unleash this potential—after all, from 2008 to
2011 the biggest driver of the recession was lower investment. The objection to this reasoning was, who would consume? Greece, after all, systematically over-consumed: in the
2000s, private consumption was 72% of GDP in Greece
versus 57% in the Eurozone.[97] Greece needed to consume
less. As the IMF noted in its March 2012 report authorizing
the country's second loan program, "domestic consumption
is expected to be suppressed for some time (this is the main
channel through which the Greek economy needs to adjust).
External demand and investor sentiment (to enable an expansion of tradables capacity) are thus crucial to a sustainable recovery in Greece."[98] In this reading, Greece could not
create growth internally. But Greece's over-consumption
was driven by imports: from 2000 to 2008, Greece's current
account deficit averaged 12.3% of GDP versus a Eurozone
average of a 1.6% surplus.[99] What Greece would need is a
shift from import-driven consumption to domestic consumption. Skeptics said, how could Greece compete with
imported goods? The point is that Greece would not compete directly—Greece doesn't have to produce an iPad or a
Mercedes. This is not how substitution works. It is not like a
household has a fixed budget for cars and decides which car
to buy—the decision-making process is more complicated

than that. And Greece can produce and offer products and services that will substitute imports in a broader rather than narrow sense.

Moving beyond a strategy of devaluation recognizes that there is more to an economy than exchange rates. Franklin Roosevelt said during the Great Depression that, "The sound internal economic system of a nation is a greater factor in its well-being than the price of its currency."[100] Flexible exchange rates are one but not the sole adjustment path. Depreciation and monetary expansion could complement other reforms, but they cannot produce productivity gains or prosperity. Instead, depreciation could easily serve as a substitute for meaningful reforms and thus replace, rather than complement, change. For the European periphery, which ranked low on competitiveness metrics, creating growth based on cheapness was too single-minded a response to their myriad problems. Ireland's prosperity in the late 1980s was based on bargain that offered "pay restraint in return for tax cuts."[101] Germany's 2000s growth combined deep reforms and a bargain with unions.[102] No country has built sustained growth through a cheap currency alone. As Anders Åslund, an economist at the Peterson Institute for International Economics, wrote in a book with the Latvian prime minister, Valdis Dombrovskis, "depreciation is an over advertised cure in current macroeconomic discourse."[103] In fact, "when a country needs to address underlying structural inefficiencies in the economy, internal devaluation is preferable to exchange rate devaluation, which offers only temporary relief from cost pressures while avoiding long overdue reforms."[104] More generally, "the prominent American macroeconomists Maurice Obstfeld and Kenneth Rogoff have pointed out 'the exceedingly weak relationship between the exchange rate and virtually any macroeconomic aggregates.' Other policies are simply more important. Therefore, the need even for major cost adjustment is not a reason to leave the euro area."[105]

Even if exiting the union could serve an individual country, it carried immense risks for the system. The Eurozone could fail or be restructured as a smaller union, but this would solve few short-term problems and create enormous uncertainty. Financial and bank exposure was only incidentally a currency problem—the underlying fear was that banks would have to write down debt, and that problem is currency-independent. The predicament would be identical if the debt were denominated in drachmas, liras, pesetas, escudos or gold. Breaking up the union, especially with minimal planning, would entail huge risks. Not because the Eurozone could not live without Greece or Portugal—it could. But an exit would trigger capital flight. If Greece exited the Eurozone, and Greek deposits were converted to drachmas at a sharp discount, Spanish and Italian depositors would have rushed to take their savings out of Spain and Italy and move them to Switzerland or Germany. Banking systems would be pressured and possibly collapse. Nor would the fallout stop there. As Åslund noted, "In the last century, Europe saw the collapse of three multi-nation currency zones, the Habsburg Empire, the Soviet Union, and Yugoslavia. They all ended in major disasters with hyperinflation. ... half the countries in a currency zone that broke up experienced hyperinflation and did not reach their prior GDP per capita in purchasing power parities until about a quarter of a century later."[106] No wonder that Åslund concluded that, "The question of how many countries would leave the EMU in this situation of grave imbalance has only two plausible answers: none or all."[107]

There would be political ramifications as well. If the euro failed, the European project would suffer a setback. Two decades of European integration will be almost undone, and the ensuing acrimony would take a long time to heal. Finger pointing on "who destroyed the euro" would dominate European politics for years, if not decades. Distrust toward Germany, France, and the European bureaucracy more broadly would delay, if not invalidate, parts of the European agenda. European politics would require a serious leadership effort to recover, and even then, a backlash against the migration of sovereignty to Brussels might undo a number of initiatives. Europe has no greater symbol than the euro. It symbolizes a peaceful, prosperous, and powerful Europe— although, more recently, also the continent's woes. A European may still envy an American who knows that the dollar is welcome currency in any corner of this earth. But Europeans could glance inside their wallets and be reminded that they inhabit an economic space with 300 million people— that they are part of a grand political and economic experiment. Remarkable given what Europe looked like 70 years ago.

Offer conditional aid. Conditional aid could not resolve the fiscal and banking crises—that would need unconditional aid to reassure markets. The argument for conditional aid rested on the proposition that meaningful reforms were an escape from the crisis. This idea rested on two observations. First, the Eurozone crisis was hardly a Eurozone-wide crisis. Countries experienced the crisis very differently. Over half the people in the Eurozone lived in countries were real GDP in 2011 was higher than in 2007, employment rates were higher and borrowing costs had declined. More than nine in ten Europeans lived in countries where GDP grew in 2011. On a regional level, unemployment in 2011 ranged from 2.5% in Salzburg and Tirol in Austria to 30.4 in Andalucía in Spain.[108] Much could be said about this crisis, but it was certainly not a uniform crisis. Given a debate about whether this crisis was the product of country-specific problems (corruption, red tape, state intervention, etc.) versus systemic flaws (common currency), the variance in outcomes made it hard to blame systemic flaws alone.

The second reason to have faith that good policy could protect a country against the crisis was that it did so in Ireland and in the Baltic countries. Ireland's robust economy did not protect it from seeking official help to begin with. Yet the IMF's raison d'être is to offer funds to countries that face liquidity problems like Ireland's. Chief among the country's problems was banking; as the IMF noted: "At the root of [Ireland's] problems is a critically-weakened banking sector that has yet to be restored to health and stands at the center of a dynamic that dampens economic recovery while creating pressures on an already serious fiscal challenge."[109] Ireland no doubt had the soundest fundamentals of all the countries that got in trouble and it only had to cope with a few problems. Ireland implemented its program diligently and its long-term interest rates fell from 12.45% in July 2011 to 5.3% in September 2012. On July 12, 2012, the IMF wrote that, "The recent notable decline in bond yields underlines the increasing confidence in Ireland's strong capacity to implement adjustment policies and also reflects the recent euro area summit statement. These developments also supported the recent successful return to the Treasury Bill market at reasonable cost."[110] Ireland's path showed that conditional aid could calm markets.

The other case study comes from the Baltic countries, which did not devalue their currencies, pursued internal devaluation by cutting wages and spending, and passed meaningful structural reforms. After a sharp contraction at the onset of the crisis, the economies of Estonia, Latvia, and Lithuania grew by 7.6%, 5.5%, and 5.9%, respectively in 2011. The governments of Estonia, Latvia, and Lithuania "did exactly what they were supposed to do and the Baltic peoples understand that, as evident from the reelection of the Estonian and Latvian governments after the crisis."[111] Here is how the IMF assessed Latvia's progress July 2012, the first reported since Latvia's bailout had ended:

Latvia's economy has emerged from the crisis more resilient and within reach of the Maastricht criteria for euro adoption, the program's exit strategy. Fiscal consolidation of more than 15 percent of GDP reduced the budget deficit to

3.5 percent of GDP ... in 2011; the current account deficit, which reached 22 percent of GDP before the crisis, declined to 1.2 percent of GDP in 2011 as the economy cooled and competitiveness improved; and the financial sector, destabilized by the collapse of Parex Bank in late-2008 and deteriorating asset quality, is well-capitalized and has returned to profitability. As a result, Latvia has been able to return to international capital markets and is well-placed to meet the Maastricht criteria.[112]

Table 8—Economic Indicators for Eurozone for 2011

Variable	Population	GDP Growth	GDP	Employment	Bonds Yields*
Unit	people	percent	(2007=100)	(2007=100)	(2007=100)
Germany	81,751,602	3.0	103.0	104.6	45.8
France	65,048,412	1.7	100.1	100.9	73.4
Italy	60,626,442	0.4	95.4	98.9	151.8
Spain	46,152,926	0.4	97.3	88.9	128.4
Netherlands	16,655,799	1.0	100.6	98.9	55.5
Greece	11,309,885	-7.1	85.4	90.7	469.8
Belgium	11,000,638	1.8	102.3	102.9	100.5
Portugal	10,572,157	-1.7	96.8	93.6	295.6
Austria	8,404,252	2.7	102.3	102.9	72.1
Slovakia	5,392,446	3.2	108.4	99.7	116.0
Finland	5,375,276	2.7	97.4	99.3	58.7
Ireland	4,569,864	1.4	93.1	85.5	202.1
Slovenia	2,050,189	0.6	97.1	95.0	152.3
Estonia	1,340,194	8.3	92.1	92.9	0.0
Cyprus	839,751	0.5	103.5	99.4	156.4
Luxembourg	511,840	1.7	99.7	110.8	50.9
Malta	415,198	1.9	106.9	107.9	93.8
Total / percent over 0 and 100	332,016,871	93%	57%	50%	54%

* Harmonized long-term interest rates for convergence assessment purposes on December 2011.
Sources: Eurostat, except bond yields from the European Central Bank

Conditional help faced two problems. The first was an overall disillusionment with markets as a whole which undermined the belief that the market would properly reward reforms. As the Pew Research Center noted in its Global Attitudes Project in July 2012,

The global economic crisis has eroded support for capitalism. In 11 of the 21 nations surveyed, half or fewer now agree with the statement that people are better off in a free market economy even though some people are rich and some are poor. And such backing is down in 9 of 16 nations with comparable data since 2007, before the Great Recession began. Such disenchantment is particularly acute in Italy (where support for a free market economy is down 23 percentage points), Spain (20 points), and Poland (15 points).[113]

The second problem was an intellectual battle against Keynesianism. Keynes argued that the process by which an economy bounces back—lower wages to induce more workers to work—does not work smoothly because workers resist decreases in nominal wages. An economy can get stuck with lower employment leading to less disposable income, less investment, and, finally, less employment. In a recession, government should borrow money and put it into people's pockets, thus accelerating the recovery. In the Eurozone, however, official aid was paired with fiscal consolidation—cuts in revenues and increases in spending, or "austerity." Keynesians argued that this was precisely the wrong medicine.

The arguments for and against Keynesianism are many and complex. From the perspective of the Eurozone, the most relevant was not whether deficit spending would stimulate growth—it would in the short term—but rather, whether it solved the underlying problems that economies faced. Deficit spending due to weak demand is diagnostically neutral, starting from an observation (low demand), but without investigating its roots. The countries in the periphery suffered from serious challenges—rigid labor markets, protected industries, and slow productivity—that need fixing. Stimulating demand is not the point. Consider this (extreme) example. Assume an economy with ten people, each of whom spent €1,000 per month. One morning, a person walks into this economy with a gun and threatens to shoot anyone who spends over €800 a month. Consumption falls by twenty percent. Then, one person disobeys and is killed.

With only nine people left, the economy now consumes on-ly €7,200, a 28% decline from its peak. On paper, an econ-omist might look at this economy and think it needs a mon-etary stimulus through lower interest rates. Or, the econo-mist could say that the government should step in and sup-port consumption directly since private consumers are not consuming. Of course, both suggestions would be absurd— what the country needs is someone to stop the guy with the gun. A Keynesian stimulus in an economy with underlying ailments is akin to trying to heat a room with an open win-dow—the heat will help, but best to close the window first.

■ ■

Greece had three options: default; default and leave the Eu-rozone; or, seek official help. Default was too dangerous and brought no appreciable short-term benefits. It would also do little to correct the underlying conditions that created the Greek crisis. Leaving the Eurozone was alluring to economists but not to either Greeks or other Europeans. Ensuring that a Greek exit did not tear apart the Eurozone would be almost impossible. Aid was the best option. But it would not be unconditional—European politics would not allow such a path. Instead, Greece traded fiscal consolida-tion and reforms for money.

The strategy hinged on the idea that crisis bred reform; as Milton Friedman said, "Only a crisis—actual or per-ceived—produces real change. When that crisis occurs, the actions that are taken depend on the ideas that are lying around."[114] Crisis would create a need for change, and the aid package aimed to ensure that the momentum was con-structive, not destructive. Yet the link between crisis and political change was never linear. Benjamin Friedman, in the *Moral Consequences of Economic Growth*, explained:

Economic growth—meaning a rising standard of living

for the clear majority of citizens—more often than not
fosters greater opportunity, tolerance of diversity, social
mobility, commitment to fairness and dedication to democracy … but when living standards stagnate or decline, most societies make little if any progress toward
any of these goals, and in all too many instances they
plainly retrogress.[115]

A recession would strain and test Greek society, stret-
ching its compassion, its tolerance, its optimism and productivity amid misery. But big crises revitalize, as the Great
Depression did in the United States in the 1930s:

> The socially corrosive power of more ordinary econom-
> ic distress is overwhelmed by still stronger forces of a
> different kind if the distress is so great as to constitute
> an out-and-out crisis, which the Great Depression cer-
> tainly was. Most people understandably exhibit generosi-
> ty when they are doing well and defensiveness when
> they are doing badly. But they nonetheless pull together
> when they see their very lives threatened and the entire
> social and political structure in which they live thrown
> into imminent danger.[116]

Weighting Greece's options and chosen path went
beyond arithmetic, though arithmetic set the context and
limits for political action. How would Greek society interp-
ret what happened to it and how would it react? What were
the ideas that lay around Greece when the crisis happened,
and would those ideas change as the crisis deepened? What
were the instincts of the political class and how did the crisis
change them? What demands did the citizenry make and
how would the system process and adjudicate those demands? What role would the troika play in politics—a positive, constructive anchor for reform, or a scapegoat, pointed
to as an excuse for Greece's ills? How could Greece create a

virtuous cycle of reform and economic growth, rather than a cycle of economic stagnation and political paralysis?

GREECE IN CRISIS

The Greek government committed to an ambitious program whose agenda implied an economic and political metamorphosis The economic agenda had three objectives: A balanced budget to lower the need to borrow money and thus make it easier to move from official aid to direct market financing; a credible path to reduce public debt and make it sustainable, so that markets trust that they will be repaid and thus start lending to Greece again; and, growth, on which improved public finances would depend. Achieving each economic objective entailed a political challenge. Bringing spending in line with taxation required a cut in spending and a rise in taxes. More taxes meant either indiscriminate taxation at the consumption level or a final end to a system of tax evasion that benefited professionals, businesses and farmers. Less spending would bring order and accountability to public finances but it would also close a spigot that politicians had used to get reelected, thus weakening the link that had connected many citizens to their representatives. Reducing public debt meant not just balanced budgets but selling state assets and privatizing (usually loss-making) state-owned enterprises. The employees in these enterprises were powerful and would mobilize against the government with a cry that Greece was "selling out" in order to enrich the rich and repay German and French bankers. Economic growth hinged on making Greece an attractive place to invest for locals and foreigners alike by increasing the flexibility of the economy to move resources to where they were needed. This meant labor reforms and the dismantling of excessive regulations for goods and services. To do all this, the Greek government needed to remain united, popular and decisive—it needed a strong mandate and it needed to do things quickly and without equivocation.

Repairing Greece's Finances

Repairing public finance was the overriding concern of the Greek government. When Greece first signed the agreement with the troika, public debt was forecasted to grow from 115% of GDP to 149% in 2012—2013 before starting to come down again to 120% by 2020. In time, the numbers changed but the 2020 target of 120—130% remained a desirable end point. To achieve it, Greece needed to turn deficits into balances, it needed to sell assets to raise money, and it needed to turn contraction into economic growth.

Table 9—Greece: Public Debt Forecasts
in percent of GDP

	2009	2010	2011	2012	2013	2014	2015	2020
First Memorandum, May 2010	115	133	145	149	149	145	139	120
First Program Review, September	115	130	139	144	144	140	134	111
Second Program Review, December	127	141	152	158	158	154	150	131
Third Program Review, March 2011	127	143	159	159	158	154	151	130
Fourth Program Review, July	127	143	166	172	170	160	146	130
Fifth Program Review, December	129	145	161	152	155	152	147	120
Second Memorandum, March 2012	129	145	165	163	167	161	153	117

Source: International Monetary Fund, Reports on Greek program

In 2009, Greece's budget deficit stood at 15.6%. How did Greece manage to run such a sizeable deficit and how did the newly elected Greek government tackle it in 2010 and 2011?

When Greece entered the Eurozone, in 2001, its overall budget was in deficit, but its primary budget (excluding interest) was in surplus. So Greece ran budget deficits, but these were driven by a need to pay interest on outstanding debt. The primary balance, which excluded interest payments, stood at a healthy 3.6% in 2000. By 2003, however, the surplus had disappeared, and the state started to borrow money not just to cover its costs but also to service debt. Public debt, which reached a low in 2003, started to climb—as a share of GDP, it grew by a third in six years (97% to 129%).

Table 10—Greece: Government Finances
in million €

Year	Revenue	Expenditure Total	Expenditure Primary	Expenditure Interest	Balance Primary	Balance Overall	Debt
2000	58,605	63,694	53,640	10,054	4,965	-5,089	140,971
2001	59,930	66,432	56,975	9,457	2,955	-6,502	151,869
2002	63,041	70,614	61,873	8,741	1,168	-7,573	159,214
2003	67,290	77,143	68,556	8,587	-1,266	-9,853	168,025
2004	70,583	84,333	75,347	8,986	-4,764	-13,750	183,187
2005	75,219	86,097	77,090	9,007	-1,871	-10,879	212,418
2006	81,844	94,407	84,629	9,778	-2,785	-12,563	224,876
2007	90,915	106,009	95,325	10,684	-4,410	-15,094	239,490
2008	94,848	117,992	106,055	11,937	-11,207	-23,144	263,284
2009	88,602	124,669	112,752	11,917	-24,150	-36,067	299,682
2010	90,232	114,302	101,109	13,193	-10,877	-24,070	329,513
2011	88,188	108,003	92,979	15,024	-4,791	-19,815	355,658
Δ: '06-'09	6,758	30,262	28,123	2,139	-21,365	-23,504	74,806
Δ: '11-'09	-414	-16,666	-19,773	3,107	19,359	16,252	55,976

as a share of GDP

Year	Revenue	Expenditure Total	Expenditure Primary	Expenditure Interest	Balance Primary	Balance Overall	Debt
2000	43.0	46.7	39.4	7.4	3.6	-3.7	103.4
2001	40.9	45.4	38.9	6.5	2.0	-4.4	103.7
2002	40.3	45.1	39.5	5.6	0.7	-4.8	101.7
2003	39.0	44.7	39.8	5.0	-0.7	-5.7	97.4
2004	38.1	45.5	40.7	4.9	-2.6	-7.4	98.9
2005	39.0	44.6	39.9	4.7	-1.0	-5.6	110.0
2006	39.2	45.2	40.5	4.7	-1.3	-6.0	107.7
2007	40.8	47.6	42.8	4.8	-2.0	-6.8	107.5
2008	40.7	50.6	45.5	5.1	-4.8	-9.9	112.9
2009	38.3	54.0	48.8	5.2	-10.5	-15.6	129.7
2010	40.6	51.5	45.5	5.9	-4.9	-10.8	148.3
2011	42.3	51.8	44.6	7.2	-2.3	-9.5	170.6
Δ: '06-'09	-0.8	8.8	8.3	0.5	-9.1	-9.6	22.0
Δ: '11-'09	3.9	-2.2	-4.2	2.0	8.2	6.1	40.9

Source: Hellenic Statistical Authority, The Greek Economy, November 2, 2012

The deteriorating fiscal position was driven, at first, by falling revenues and, after that, by a rise in spending. As a share of GDP, revenues were at an all-time high in 2000—at no other point in Greek history did the state collect as much as it did in 2000. Once in the Eurozone, Greece's discipline on tax collection weakened, and revenue fell. In 2000, the "percentage of collected revenue to assessed [revenue]" was 89.5%, a number that shrunk to 74.6% in 2006, evidence of an inability to even collect taxes that it was owed.[1] The country then passed tax reforms that reduced total revenues to their 1997 level. Between 2004 and 2009, revenues fluctuated within a band of 38—41% of GDP, but they never surpassed the 2000 peak. In 2009, an election year and the start of the economic crisis, revenues were at their second lowest point in a decade.

Spending, however, boomed. From 2000 to 2006, primary spending was more or less flat, but as Greece entered the Eurozone, it was able to refinance its debt at lower interest rates, and so its cost to service debt declined by a third. Even in 2010, as the crisis was intensifying, Greece spent less on servicing debt than it did in 2001. At first, the reduction in debt service brought down the government's total expenditure. But from 2007 onward, primary spending started to rise again. By 2009, it had increased almost by a fifth relative to GDP, and by a third in nominal terms, from €84.6 billion to €112.7 billion.

The 2009 budget deficit was thus driven mostly by rising expenditure. Between 2006 and 2009, the balance worsened by 9.6 percentage points; of that change, lower revenues accounted for 0.8 and higher interest payments accounted for 0.5 points. Primary spending made up the remaining 8.3 points. The 2009 budget deficit was a spending-driven deficit.

The 2009—2011 adjustment shrank the overall deficit from 15.6% to 9.5%. The fiscal adjustment was driven as much by revenues (+3.9) as by spending (-4.2). Higher interest payments brought debt service to its highest level since 2001. The economy, however, was shrinking in 2009—2011, and so it is useful to look at the absolute numbers in addition to the numbers relative to GDP. To achieve the overall deficit reduction of €16.2 billion from 2009 to 2011, revenues remained broadly flat, spending fell by almost €20 billion, and interest payments increased by €3.1 billion. On a nominal basis, then, the 2009—2011 adjustment was driven more by spending rather than revenue.

Table 11—Greece: Government Revenues
in million €

Year	Total Revenue	Taxes on production and imports	Taxes on income and property	Social contributions	Other	Capital transfers
2000	58,605	18,569	13,158	16,989	5,955	3,934
2001	59,930	19,519	12,528	18,397	7,341	2,145
2002	63,041	20,159	13,415	21,310	6,237	1,920
2003	67,290	20,756	13,498	23,722	6,365	2,949
2004	70,583	21,637	14,825	24,671	6,360	3,090
2005	75,219	22,753	16,589	26,104	6,694	3,079
2006	81,844	25,948	16,975	25,942	7,825	5,154
2007	90,915	28,425	18,219	28,962	9,588	5,721
2008	94,848	28,985	18,714	30,749	11,164	5,236
2009	88,602	26,153	19,146	29,457	10,609	3,237
2010	90,232	27,345	17,515	29,764	11,001	4,607
2011	88,188	26,635	18,031	27,492	11,071	4,959
Δ: '06-'09	6,758	205	2,171	3,515	2,784	-1,917
Δ: '11-'09	-414	482	-1,115	-1,965	462	1,722

as a share of GDP

Year	Total Revenue	Taxes on production and imports	Taxes on income and property	Social contributions	Other	Capital transfers
2000	43.0	13.6	9.7	12.5	4.4	2.9
2001	40.9	13.3	8.6	12.6	5.0	1.5
2002	40.3	12.9	8.6	13.6	4.0	1.2
2003	39.0	12.0	7.8	13.8	3.7	1.7
2004	38.1	11.7	8.0	13.3	3.4	1.7
2005	39.0	11.8	8.6	13.5	3.5	1.6
2006	39.2	12.4	8.1	12.4	3.7	2.5
2007	40.8	12.8	8.2	13.0	4.3	2.6
2008	40.7	12.4	8.0	13.2	4.8	2.2
2009	38.3	11.3	8.3	12.7	4.6	1.4
2010	40.6	12.3	7.9	13.4	5.0	2.1
2011	42.3	12.8	8.6	13.2	5.3	2.4
Δ: '06-'09	-0.8	-1.1	0.2	0.3	0.8	-1.1
Δ: '11-'09	3.9	1.5	0.4	0.4	0.7	1.0

Source: Hellenic Statistical Authority, The Greek Economy, November 2, 2012

On the revenue side, the decline in 2000—2004 came from reductions across the board. Taxes on production and imports declined by two percentage points, on income and property by almost two points and capital transfers (chiefly EU financing for the public investment budget) by more than one percentage point. Only social contributions increased. From 2004 to 2009, most variables moved within a narrow band, and revenues in 2009 were almost identical as a fraction of income as in 2004 (both election years, however, and both saw a yearly decline relative to the previous year). Then, as the crisis hit, and the government tried to close the budget deficit, there was a sizable change in the composition of revenues. Taxes on income and social contributions declined in absolute terms, due to the recession which decimated incomes, employment and profits, but they increased relative to GDP, due to the government's efforts to sustain revenues in the midst of the crisis. The two largest contributors to revenues were increases in taxes on production and imports and increases in capital transfers. The former came courtesy of extraordinary taxation on consumption, chiefly on value added and gasoline taxes. The rationale was both fiscal—to raise revenue—but also technical: taxes on consumption are easier to collect and harder to evade. While the government implemented measures to tackle tax evasion, consumption taxes would provide additional funding to the treasury until the benefits of reduced evasion materialized. Higher capital transfers were partly a correction from an abnormally low value in 2009, and they came exclusively from higher EU funding for the public investment budget, which rose from a low of €1.8 billion in 2009 to €3.6 billion in 2011.[2] Combined, these measures held nominal revenues flat, but they pushed them to a ten-year high as a share of GDP. Since the revenue in 2000 was an all-time high, in the midst of the economic crisis, in 2011, the Greek government collected about as much revenue as ever before in its history. Revenue might have been a long-term problem, but it was not an aberration in 2011.

On the other side of the budget, more than three-fourths of the 2006—2009 increase in spending was driven by higher social benefits (chiefly, pensions) and wages for government employees. The 2009—2011 drop, however, did not come from the same sources. Of the 4.2 percentage point adjustment, the two most important items were lower "goods and services" and lower "capital transfers." The former was partly due to a decline in weapons procurement, which fell by 83% in two years (€2,175 to €359 million).[3] The latter came from a shrinking public investment budget (-€2,980 million) for transportation, industry, and regional development.[4] Fewer weapons and less investment accounted for a quarter of the spending adjustment. Wages fell by €5 billion (-16.4%) due to a smaller civil service and lower wages. In 2009—2011, the civil service shrank by ~56,000 (-7.8%),[5] so half the decline in the wage bill came from letting people retire (or not renewing short-term contracts) rather than lower wages. As a share of GDP, spending on wages remained higher than in any year before 2008. The only spending item that increased, as a share of GDP, was "social benefits" which not only rose, but reached an all time high. In part, this could have been due to counter-cyclical spending for unemployment benefits, although there is no evidence for this hypothesis: unemployment benefits fell in 2009—2010, and the social budget is anyway driven by pensions, sickness and disability payments, which together accounted for over three-fourths of total spending in 2009—2010.[6] More likely is a rise in the number of pensioners (together with pension spending, of course). From the mid 1980s, the number of "pensioners receiving principal pension from the social insurance organizations" had averaged 76% of the total population over 65. Within a year, from 2007 to 2008, it jumped to 82%, the highest rate ever.[7] One explanation was that pension reforms in 2008 pushed a lot of people to early retirement for fear that their upcoming benefits could be jeopardized, creating a fiscal dynamic that was hard to contain once the crisis started.

Table 12—Greece: Government Expenditures
in million €

Year	Total Spending	Primary Spending	Wages	Social benefits	Goods and services	Capital transfers	Other	Interest payments
2000	63,694	53,640	14,270	20,155	8,778	8,789	1,648	10,054
2001	66,432	56,975	15,180	22,499	9,063	8,482	1,751	9,457
2002	70,614	61,873	17,308	24,184	10,229	8,384	1,768	8,741
2003	77,143	68,556	18,641	27,332	10,387	9,565	2,631	8,587
2004	84,333	75,347	21,345	28,873	10,155	11,313	3,661	8,986
2005	86,097	77,090	22,384	31,814	10,884	8,430	3,578	9,007
2006	94,407	84,629	23,334	35,625	12,387	9,767	3,516	9,778
2007	106,009	95,325	25,464	39,941	15,030	11,115	3,775	10,684
2008	117,992	106,055	28,000	45,758	15,046	13,212	4,039	11,937
2009	124,669	112,752	31,010	48,972	17,111	11,985	3,674	11,917
2010	114,302	101,109	27,773	47,220	13,679	8,888	3,549	13,193
2011	108,003	92,979	25,938	47,210	9,881	7,234	2,716	15,024
Δ: '06-'09	30,262	28,123	7,676	13,347	4,724	2,218	158	2,139
Δ: '11-'09	-16,666	-19,773	-5,072	-1,762	-7,230	-4,751	-958	3,107

as a share of GDP

Year	Total Spending	Primary Spending	Wages	Social benefits	Goods and services	Capital transfers	Other	Interest payments
2000	46.7	39.4	10.5	14.8	6.4	6.4	1.2	7.4
2001	45.4	38.9	10.4	15.4	6.2	5.8	1.2	6.5
2002	45.1	39.5	11.1	15.4	6.5	5.4	1.1	5.6
2003	44.7	39.8	10.8	15.9	6.0	5.5	1.5	5.0
2004	45.5	40.7	11.5	15.6	5.5	6.1	2.0	4.9
2005	44.6	39.9	11.6	16.5	5.6	4.4	1.9	4.7
2006	45.2	40.5	11.2	17.1	5.9	4.7	1.7	4.7
2007	47.6	42.8	11.4	17.9	6.7	5.0	1.7	4.8
2008	50.6	45.5	12.0	19.6	6.5	5.7	1.7	5.1
2009	54.0	48.8	13.4	21.2	7.4	5.2	1.6	5.2
2010	51.5	45.5	12.5	21.3	6.2	4.0	1.6	5.9
2011	51.8	44.6	12.4	22.6	4.7	3.5	1.3	7.2
Δ: '06-'09	8.8	8.3	2.2	4.1	1.5	0.5	-0.1	0.5
Δ: '11-'09	-2.2	-4.2	-1.0	1.4	-2.7	-1.7	-0.3	2.0

Source: Hellenic Statistical Authority, The Greek Economy, November 2, 2012

The fiscal adjustment of 2009—2011 was thus both a revenue and a spending adjustment. On the revenue side, it consisted of higher taxes on consumption and a reversion of EU financing from an abnormally point in 2009 back to its historical levels. Together with measures to boost tax collection, revenues as a share of GDP almost reached an all-time high in 2011 (second only to 2000). Spending declined from a contraction in the number of civil servants, a decline in public investment and a drop in weapons procurement— over sixty percent of the €19.8 billion fall in primary spending came from these three sources. Social benefits declined in absolute but not in relative terms. In 2011, social spending was at a historical peak, and spending on wages was higher than any point before 2008. After two years of adjustments, the primary deficit was down, but revenues were at record levels and so were expenditures.

Growth in the Age of Austerity

How did this fiscal consolidation impact the real economy? Analysts both in and outside Greece argued that it was killing it—spending cuts lowered demand, and tax hikes shrank disposable income, creating a contraction in economic activity. The contraction, in turn, lowered revenues, forcing the government to pass new measures, and thus repeating and worsening the vicious cycle. This argument had enormous intellectual appeal, but little basis in reality. It was an inadequate description of what was happening in Greece. The recession started in late 2008 and it deepened in 2009. Yet the period 2007—2009 marked the largest expansion in state spending since the 1980s. The recession caused austerity, not the other way around, at least not until later. What happened?

Before austerity and before Lehman Brothers, Greece's housing bubble burst. This was the third housing boom-and-bust in the country's history. Investment in construction was rising rapidly before the crisis at 10% a year from 2000 to 2006. The Bank of Greece reported the price of urban dwellings peaked in 2008 at 89% above 2000 levels, which was more modest relative to other housing bubbles.[8] The increase of 19% from 2003 to 2007 in Greece (as reported by the OECD) was below the increase in Spain (+37%), Ireland (+36%), or France (+46%).[9] Even in 2007, construction of buildings was below its 2005 peak. Gross fixed capital formation in dwellings peaked in 2006 and that of "other buildings and structures" in 2009, meaning that investment in civil engineering projects was counter-cyclical to the investment in dwellings—falling in 2005—2007, when spending in dwellings rose, and recovering in 2008—

2010 when investment in dwellings collapsed.[10] Employment in construction fell by half from Q2 2008 to Q2 2012, and of all the people who lost their jobs in that time, one in four came from construction.

Table 13—Greece: National Accounts
in constant million € of 2005

Year	GDP	Private Consumption	Government Consumption	Gross capital formation	Exports	Imports
2000	158,907	109,373	31,166	37,438	39,527	-58,597
2001	165,360	114,806	31,398	38,908	39,522	-59,274
2002	170,990	120,252	33,666	39,399	36,205	-58,532
2003	181,244	124,189	33,373	46,687	37,262	-60,267
2004	189,107	128,952	34,547	45,578	43,712	-63,682
2005	193,050	134,725	34,937	41,322	44,807	-62,741
2006	203,681	140,595	36,017	50,042	46,739	-69,712
2007	210,978	145,644	38,575	56,513	50,066	-79,820
2008	210,434	151,852	37,559	50,662	50,898	-80,537
2009	203,609	149,476	39,398	37,982	41,015	-64,262
2010	193,801	140,138	35,988	34,831	43,142	-60,298
2011	179,972	129,321	34,129	29,110	43,283	-55,871

Yearly change. in constant million € of 2005

Year	GDP	Private Consumption	Government Consumption	Gross capital formation	Exports	Imports
2000						
2001	6,453	5,433	232	1,470	-5	-677
2002	5,630	5,446	2,268	491	-3,317	742
2003	10,254	3,937	-293	7,288	1,057	-1,735
2004	7,863	4,763	1,174	-1,109	6,450	-3,415
2005	3,943	5,773	390	-4,256	1,095	941
2006	10,631	5,870	1,080	8,720	1,932	-6,971
2007	7,297	5,049	2,558	6,471	3,327	-10,108
2008	-544	6,208	-1,016	-5,851	832	-717
2009	-6,825	-2,376	1,839	-12,680	-9,883	16,275
2010	-9,808	-9,338	-3,410	-3,151	2,127	3,964
2011	-13,829	-10,817	-1,859	-5,721	141	4,427

Note: Revised data after 2005 (break in series). Totals as reported. Source: Hellenic Statistical Authority, The Greek Economy, November 2, 2012

In 2009, thus, the economy was contracting because investment, chiefly in construction, was plummeting.[11] Industrial production fell by a sixth, and exports declined by a fifth driven by a sharp decline in net receipts from shipping that reflected the reduction in global demand.[12] The only "positive" was the collapse of imports (which, from an accounting perspective, added to GDP). By 2009, private consumption had declined only modestly (-1.6%). Until 2009, this was a business, not a household recession.

The composition of the recession changed again in 2010. Output fell by 4.9%. Private consumption led the way with a 6.3% drop, bringing real consumption down below its 2006 level. Investment continued its free fall, this time driven mostly by construction and other machinery and equipment (other means excluding transport). Exports registered an uptick, but this mostly came from a 62% increase in exports of oil products (as domestic demand plummeted, refiners exported their products rather than sell in the local market).[13] Imports also fell but by a much smaller amount than in 2010 (-6%). Government consumption also fell by 8.7%, although this item in the national account only covers a fraction of total government spending. In 2011, the recession became even more heavily driven by private consumption (-7.7%), although the decline in investment also accelerated (-16.4%). The export boom of 2010 was over, although imports continued to shrink. GDP fell by 7.1%.

The industries that most analysts hoped would generate growth were tourism and shipping. Both disappointed.

Tourism. Greece has never had a problem attracting tourists. The number of people visiting Greece grew by 2.2% a year from 2005 to 2011. Interestingly, the composition of those visitors changed in that time period. In 2005, 50% of the visitors came from the Eurozone; by 2011, that share had dropped to 40%. There was also a (more modest) decline in visitors from EU counties outside the Eurozone. These declines, however, were more than offset by a big increase (10% a year) in arrivals from other countries (Russia, Israel, Turkey, and the Balkans). This number seems to contradict the idea that an appreciation in the Euro made Greece less attractive as a destination—in fact, tourism from Eurozone countries fell while tourism from other countries increased. More worryingly, however, Greece's market share was declining. In 2005, Greece's global market share was 1.8%, and that declined to 1.7% in 2011. Its market share in

Southern Europe also declined from 9.4% in 2005 to 9% in 2011. So while Greece was receiving more tourists, it was not keeping up with the growth in global or regional tourism.

The bigger problem, however, was quality, not quantity. Greece earned as much from tourism in 2011 as it did in 2005 (modest decline). So while tourism made up 21% of exports in 2005, it made up just 18.6% in 2011 (continuing a steady decline from 25% in 2000). What is more, a euro in 2011 bought less than a euro in 2005: when controlling for inflation, Greece's 2011 receipts were 20% lower than in 2005. Given that Greece was receiving more tourists, lower revenues were the result of value (how much tourists spent) rather than volume (how many came). Tourists in 2011 spent 14% less time in Greece than in 2005; meanwhile, they spent as much per night as they did in the past—but only on a nominal basis. On a real basis, spending per night fell by 18% relative to 2005.

Table 14—Greece: Tourism Statistics

	2005	2006	2007	2008	2009	2010	2011	2005=100
Visitors (000s)	14,388	15,226	16,165	15,939	14,915	15,007	16,427	114
Eurozone	7,069	7,591	7,595	7,174	6,599	6,109	6,600	93
EU ex. Eurozone	4,149	4,320	4,867	4,642	4,289	4,091	4,098	99
Others	3,170	3,316	3,703	4,124	4,027	4,808	5,729	181
Market Share (% Global)	1.8	1.8	1.8	1.7	1.7	1.6	1.7	93
Market Share (% S. Europe)	9.4	8.9	9.1	9.3	9.1	8.9	9.0	96
Receipts (€ 000 nominal)	10,730	11,357	11,319	11,636	10,400	9,611	10,505	98
Receipts (€ 000 real 2005)	10,730	10,993	10,638	10,492	9,253	8,167	8,657	81
Receipts (% of exports)	20.8	20.7	18.9	17.5	20.0	17.9	18.6	89
# nights / visitor	10.66	10.65	9.97	9.57	9.48	9.34	9.19	86
€ spent / night (nominal)	69.7	70.0	70.2	76.3	73.5	68.6	69.6	100
€ spent / night (real 2005)	69.7	67.8	66.0	68.8	65.4	58.3	57.3	82

Source: Bank of Greece, Eurostat, UN World Tourism Organization, Author's calculations

These numbers showed that Greece was able to receive more tourists, although its market share declined. The deeper problem was an inability to keep tourists longer or to charge them more. Insofar as goods and services cost more due to inflation, the result was that tourists bought less—on a nominal basis, they spent as much per night as in 2005. Greece was unable to extract more from tourists either by offering them higher value services or by providing them with more things to do, which would make them spend more time in Greece.

Shipping. Besides tourism, shipping is among Greece's most important exports, affecting the Greek economy through numerous channels. In terms of the trade balance, shipping counts both as a good and a service—the former refers to the buying and selling of ships, while the latter deals with maritime. The shipping balance is a function of four pieces: (a) the money sent abroad to buy ships versus (b) the revenues generated from the selling of ships; and (c) the money earned by providing maritime services versus (d) the money spent to purchase maritime services (e.g., at ports, logistics, repairs, etc.).

Table 15—*Greece: Shipping Market*

	Goods balance (a+b)	Ship sales (a)	Ship purchases (b)	Services balance (c+d)	Receipts (c)	Payments (d)	Net (a+b+c+d)	# Ships (~March)	DWT, millions
2002	435	531	-97	4,006	7,997	-3,992	4,440	3,480	165
2003	136	261	-124	5,143	8,961	-3,818	5,280	3,355	172
2004	136	1,291	-1,156	7,918	12,404	-4,486	8,054	3,370	180
2005	-723	1,602	-2,325	8,306	12,953	-4,647	7,583	3,338	183
2006	-3,391	1,632	-5,022	8,256	13,280	-5,025	4,865	3,397	190
2007	-5,520	2,275	-7,796	10,252	15,679	-5,427	4,731	3,699	218
2008	-4,705	1,582	-6,287	11,139	17,624	-6,485	6,434	4,173	261
2009	-3,357	772	-4,129	7,472	12,262	-4,790	4,115	4,161	264
2010	-3,621	799	-4,420	8,088	14,013	-5,925	4,467	3,996	258
2011	-3,261	755	-4,016	7,630	12,711	-5,081	4,369	3,848	262

Source: Bank of Greece, Hellenic Chamber of Shipping

Looking at maritime service exports alone (c), there was in fact a boom—at the peak in 2008, the Greek economy exported €17.6 billion worth of maritime services, a near doubling versus 2002 (€8 billion). But in net terms, the contribution to the current account grew from €4.4 billion in 2002 to €6.4 billion in 2008; by 2011, the net balance from shipping was at the same level as in 2002 in nominal terms, in part because, as the global economy started to slow down and shipping charter rates declined, the revenues from shipping fell to their 2004-2005 levels.

The discrepancy between the top line number (receipts) and the net number comes from two sources. First, Greek ship-owners expanded their fleets, prompting a capital out-flow to pay for these ships. In nominal terms, between 2002 and 2011, ship-owners spent almost €35 billion to buy ships—they also, however, earned around €11.5 billion by selling them. So in the period from 2002 to 2011, Greece spent a net of €23.8 billion on ships—around €2.4 billion a year. The total number of ships under Greek control grew by 10% in that period, although the deadweight tonnage grew by a much greater 59%, which means that Greeks bought bigger ships. And second, the Greek shipping indus-try also increased its purchases of maritime services from abroad (d): from €4 billion in 2002 to almost €6.5 billion in 2008 (at the peak), before falling to €5.1 billion in 2011.

These numbers show a more nuanced role for Greek shipping in terms of the current account. The peak contri-bution came in 2004 and 2005 when charter rates were ris-ing (see receipts) but before the Greek shipping industry started a massive fleet expansion program, which started in 2006 (where ship purchases doubled from €2.3 billion to €5 billion). Once the fleet expansion began, the contribution to the current account shrank. In fact, in 2007, at the height of the commodity boom, the contribution to the Greek current account was lower than it was in 2003. By 2011, the net bal-ance was at its 2002 level.

Privatizations: Big Targets, Disappointing Results

One way for Greece to pay down debt was by exploiting public assets and engaging in privatizations. From May 2010 to March 2012, Greece and the troika revised the country's privatization targets six times, ranging from a total amount raised of €5 billion to €50 billion. How did those numbers come about? Why did the troika think that Greece could raise €50 billion in a five-year period?

The point of departure was Greece's assets. In its De-cember 2010 review of the program, the IMF showed a ta-ble with what Greece owned: €12 billion in currency, €2 billion in securities, €1 billion in loans, €39 billion in shares, €21 billion in other financial assets, and €120 billion in public sector capital stock. There was also an "n/a" entry for real estate, pending a study, but the IMF noted that analysts had put these holdings at €200–€300 billion. So the Greek state had €330 billion in debt and some €500 billion in assets.[14]

Table 16—Greece: Privatization Receipts Targets

in billion €

	2011	2012	2013	2014	2015	2016	Total
First Memorandum (May 2010)	1.0	1.0	1.0	1.0	1.0		5.0
Second Program Review (December 2010)	1.0	2.0	2.0	2.0	2.0		9.0
Third Program Review (March 2011)	2.5	3.0	3.0	2.0	2.0		12.5
Fourth Program Review (July 2011)	3.0	7.5	11.0	13.5	15.0		50.0
Fifth Program Review (December 2011)	1.0	5.9	14.0	14.1	5.0	5.0	45.0
Second Memorandum (March 2012)	1.0	3.2	4.3	4.4	5.7	5.9	24.5

Source: International Monetary Fund, Reports on Greek program

Merely selling assets to pay down debt was not an ideal strategy, but using underutilized or unutilized assets could have alleviated the country's dire fiscal position. What is more, from 1991 to 2009, Greece raised $29.2 billion from privatizations, and from 2005 to 2009, it had raised $2.9 billion a year.[15] In other words, the first three targets assumed a continuation of pre-crisis sale trends. Of course, in a crisis, prices would likely be depressed, but the initial privatization targets were just business as usual.

As the country's privatization goal edged up, the IMF supported its targets with more evidence. In its March 2011 review, the IMF noted that the target for Greece to raise €50 billion from asset sales "would be at the high end of the pace that other countries have in the past managed to adhere to." The IMF pointed to five episodes of large privatizations: Peru, Estonia, Argentina, Hungary, and Greece. Each privatization effort was a multi-year affair, ranging from 4 years (Peru) to 8 years (Hungary). These countries were able to raise annual proceeds of anywhere from 1.8%

of GDP to as high as 4% of GDP, for a cumulative effect of 11.1% to 32% of GDP. By contrast, noted the IMF, Greece's target would entail a five-year effort to raise 4% of GDP in annual proceeds and 20% of average GDP. Hard but doable.[16]

This data, of course, was very narrow, drawing from only five episodes, all of them in the 1990s. Yet a fuller analysis of privatizations in 23 European countries since 1981 showed similar results:

- On average, countries were able to raise 1.08% of GDP through privatizations.
- Around half (47%) of the observations involved privatizations where countries raised over 0.5% of GDP; in those cases, proceeds averaged 1.78% of GDP.
- Around a quarter (26%) of the observations involved privatizations where countries raised over 1% of GDP; in those cases, proceeds averaged 2.51% of GDP.
- Around 18% of the observations involved countries that were experiencing a recession.
- Only 4.4% of the observations involved countries that were able to raise over 4% of GDP annually through privatizations.[17]

These numbers showed that the targets were ambitious but not outrageous. But should privatizations have been a priority? Answering that question was a difficult economic and political exercise—and one which Greece's politicians avoided.

First, there is no doubt that the state has legitimate interests which markets will not fulfill on their own. For example, flying regularly to a remote island may not be a profitable proposition and one that the market will not provide at sufficient quantities. Yet a state has an interest in ensuring that all its citizens are connected. This is just one example. Markets will no doubt fail to provide certain goods and services that a state should want provided.

Second, private companies tend to be better managed, but not all state owned enterprises (SOEs) are inefficient—some (but not many) are indeed world class. Nor are private companies perfect—many lose money and engage in harmful or outright criminal behavior. Left unsupervised, private companies can undermine the public interest. We should neither dismiss public companies nor idolize private ones: believing in private or public enterprise should be an empirical, not an ideological position.

Third, the agent-principal problem applies to both public and private companies. Companies are meant to serve their shareholders, but they often serve their managers and employees instead. This happens due to information asymmetries, perverse incentives, and a pure inability to control a company's day-to-day operations. Therefore, not every decision will be in the interests of the company's shareholders, whether these are private investors or the state.

What then distinguishes private from public ownership? The most important difference is the possibility of failure. If a company cannot compete, it will go bankrupt. In private enterprise, this is a constructive force and allows resources to move from unproductive to productive uses. But SOEs rarely go bust. For one, states often own companies because they do not think that profit is their chief function—instead, they are presumed to serve some public interest. Rather than shut down unprofitable SOEs, states recapitalize them and socialize their losses. Even if states want to shut them down, they may not be able to due to social pressures. If a car factory cannot make money, people may protest its closure but there is nothing they can do about it. But they can petition a government—and vote-hungry governments often listen to those petitions.

Why is this problematic? First, the absence of failure

distorts incentives. Without failure, an SOE has little incentive to invest, to offer superior services, or to keep costs down. Survival depends on political connections. Therefore, the company no longer serves its customers (their view does not matter) or the state in a broader sense. Instead, SOEs need to cater to political interests to keep the money flowing. At a minimum, this structure creates bad products and services.

The second problem is that such behavior distorts the markets in which the public company operates. SOEs tend to dislike competition since it underlines their own inferior goods or services. Who wants to work for the company that has 30-year-old planes when your competitors have shiny, new planes? Competition separates the good from the bad. Thus, state companies tend to lobby the governments for restrictions and regulations in their industry and they can even directly undercut competition by offering very low prices (as losing money is not a problem).

Of course, these efforts are couched in the name of consumers' or the public interest—they are presented as a concern for prices or reliability in "strategic" sectors. Almost always, these arguments are a sham: instead, state companies want to protect their own privileges and will do anything to do so, including undermining other companies that can deliver the same service more cheaply and reliably. Consumers not only get bad services but they are also likely to be prevented from a chance to get the same service from private providers.

The third problem is that the inability to shut down companies has costs. When the state puts money into SOEs, it does so by either taxing people or borrowing money on their behalf. There is no free lunch: people pay for these companies either directly (by buying their products) or indirectly (by financing the state). A train ticket may cost €15 but if the state-owned railroad company runs a deficit financed by the state, the real price is above €15—and in fact, people who do not use this service subsidize the people who do.

In that process, however, the state loses sight of costs and benefits. Greek state owned enterprises lost €1.2 billion in 2011. Is what Greece got in return worth €1.2 billion? Is it worth €1.9 billion (what they lost in 2010)?[18] These questions become very hard to answer. It is easy for a person to ask, do I want to pay €150 to fly from Athens to Thessaloniki? But when there are hidden costs, it is harder to compare costs with benefits, and cost-benefit analysis becomes too opaque.

These critiques prompt a question: can the state safeguard its interests without owning a company? Take the example of the unprofitable flight route mentioned above—clearly there is a state interest and clearly the market will under-provide this service. But the state has many ways to deal with this. It can, on one extreme, own a company so that it can directly provide this service. Or it can merely pay a private provider an amount that will make that provider want to supply this service. In a perfect world, the burden of the two options would be the same. But this is not a perfect world and so the difference ends up being much higher under direct ownership. Or the state can impose regulations on the private sector—make the right to fly contingent on servicing these unprofitable routes. There is a wide spectrum of options and owning a company is an extreme and costly way of getting something done.

So far, this is generic analysis, although given a natural suspicion toward markets, it is never a bad idea to restate the basic principles. Let us now turn to Greece. Most SOEs in Greece lose money—that, in itself, is a case for privatizing them. But financial results should not be the sole factor. Assume that Athens had an amazing metro but the company lost €1 a year; should the company be privatized? Maybe not. Maybe €1 a year is a tolerable subsidy for a perfect metro, even though the private sector could have probably offered better service. At the same time, we ought to ask ourselves, is this result sustainable? Can the company open new stations and invest in new trains if it does not make money? If not, then maybe it should be privatized.

Conversely, let's assume that a company generated profits—is that an argument against privatization? For one, if it has a monopoly, profits are easy. The company may also be "milking" old assets—it can earn a profit but it does not have enough money to invest. Imagine this: let's say I own a newspaper and one day all the journalists quit and I replace them with third-rate journalists. For a while, this can remain a profitable company, because it will be a while before advertisers pull out and subscribers stop buying the paper. Short-term profits may even go up because costs went down (by hiring cheaper staff). But current profitability masks an inevitable decline.

In Greece, the case for privatizations rested on four pillars. The first and most obvious was financial. Greece could no longer afford to subsidize companies. These companies would no longer have funds to carry out their essential duties. In June 2012, for example, the power company secured loans for €525 million with interest rates ranging from 7+ to 11.9%. In that environment, the company's ability to keep going was severely impaired.

Second, SOEs tend to be inefficient and provide services at a higher cost than private companies could. Even if the state could afford to subsidize SOEs, it shouldn't. The most glaring evidence comes from data published by the Ministry of Finance showing that salaries at SOEs were twice as high as the average salary in the private sector in 2008. This was hard to justify on productivity or other bases. The taxpayer was paying a lot of money extra for services that tend to be substandard.

Third, privatizations were an essential component of broader market opening and deregulation. The power market is a perfect example again: as long as the power company retained its current form, competitive markets would be impossible to form. It would be hard to achieve more competition and lower prices without also changing the ownership of what is usually the biggest or the only company in an industry. What was true for power was true for other sectors.

Fourth, Greece needed to signal its commitment to change. Privatizations tend to be politically tough, especially in countries such as Greece, where skepticism of markets and the power of labor unions are high. No wonder many analysts saw privatizations as a barometer for government resolve. Delayed privatizations increased skepticism that Greece could change.

Experience teaches us three things about how to privatize. First, the process of selling assets should be fair and transparent. Second, privatization needs to be accompanied with a broader market opening—there is no sense in turning a public into a private monopoly. And third, privatizations require regulation: functions that were previously either not needed or performed by SOEs will be now performed by the state. To do this the state needs to upgrade its capacity to regulate these new industries and to ensure that market competition is indeed serving the public interest.

The most serious and perhaps only objection to the case for privatizations was timing. Greece was unlikely to get a great value for its assets; why sell now rather than wait? This was a legitimate concern, even though realistically Greece cannot afford to wait. But there was a different way to ask this question: Could Greece achieve its economic and political goals without privatizations? Could it reinforce a sense of justice that it was willing to stand up to labor unions? Could it put its public debt on a sustainable path? Could it open up industries to attract investment? Could it communicate domestically and internationally a serious willingness to liberalize the economy? Could it do any of these things without privatizations? Probably not—and that is what made privatizations essential.

The Papandreou Premiership—and its Collapse

In October 2009, George Papandreou was elected prime minister on the back of a corruption scandal that swept aside the conservatives after a five-year reign, their longest in power since the late 1970s. Lehman Brothers had just gone bankruptcy (mid September), so the campaign took place mostly in the milder part of the global financial crisis, at least relative to what came next. Yet Papandreou made one comment in that campaign, less than a month before the election, which would haunt him throughout his term: "there is money," he said. In part, the quote was taken out of context. Lamenting the inability of the conservative government to attract EU funds for clean energy, he said: "They keep asking us, 'where will you find the money?' There is money—if we fight for it, if we attract it with investments, if we tidy up the state, if we utilize the productive forces of our country so that they can create new wealth."[19] The subtext was soon lost. But context was only part of the issue. Data accuracy was the other. The 2009 budget deficit was revised multiple times, and the final estimate was four times higher than the first one. Only after the election was Greece's fiscal hole fully understood, and it took another year for the "final" numbers to come in. As one IMF official noted: "Our people went in and couldn't believe what they found … The way they were keeping track of their finances—they knew how much they had agreed to spend, but no one was keeping track of what he had actually spent. It wasn't even what you would call an emerging economy. It was a Third World country."[20] No matter the pre-election agenda, Papandreou's new task was to save Greece.

Crisis management took a toll on the government's popularity, and it alienated the public which felt angry and powerless. When Papandreou was elected, eight in ten Greeks viewed him positively. As he resigned two years later only one in ten did. Papandreou's loss was no one's gain. For most of the crisis, almost a third of the electorate endorsed no party and claimed it would abstain if elections were held. Growing unpopularity raised the pressure for holding fresh elections. In January 2011, fewer than one in six wanted early elections; by the time elections were called in March 2012, two-thirds wanted them. Greece was not being saved.

Papandreou was a clumsy politician. Thrice he dragged the country into a circus for no apparent reason—he was then forced to resign. The November 2010 local elections were the first political test for the PASOK government, coming just six months after the bailout agreement. Local elections had always been seen as a gauge for public opinion, even though local issue matter as much as national politics. Yet the prime minister said he considered the elections to be a referendum on his premiership and on the bailout agreement—vote for us or else we will go to polls to elect a new national government, he threatened. Raising massively the stakes, the statement caught people by surprise. He then took an ambiguous first-round result and declared victory, making no mention of the threat to hold elections. In the run-off election, a week later, the abstention rate climbed to almost two-thirds. The sentiment was: "We will not vote against you because we do not want elections, but we will not vote for you either because you are just as much to blame for this mess."

Papandreou created another political crisis in June 2011. As the year progressed it was clear that Greece would miss some of its budget targets, and so the government introduced a set of spending cuts and tax hikes that were collectively labeled the "medium-term strategy." In the face of protest and violence, the prime minister reportedly offered to the leader of the opposition to step down in favor of a government of national unity ("If I am the problem, I will go," he reportedly told the leader of the opposition). A few hours later, in a nationally televised address, he backtracked, blaming the opposition for leaking his conversation with the opposition leader to the press. Instead, he announced a cabinet reshuffle and a vote of confidence from parliament. The reshuffle elevated the prime minister's chief rival, Evangelos Venizelos, to the post of finance minister, and helped the party to close ranks. Yet the theatrics of the affair damaged the prime minister. Papandreou's popularity fell, the main opposition party surpassed PASOK in the polls for the first time, and the number of people who thought elections were needed registered its sharpest uptick from 22% in May 2011 to 37% in July 2011. As in the local elections ultimatum of November 2010, the public felt that Papandreou had played too much politics.

The third crisis that Papandreou created—and which ended his political career—came just as he had negotiated a second bailout and a debt restructuring with the private sector (haircut) in October 2011. A haircut, as any woman knows, can be rejuvenating or it can be a disaster. In Greece's case, the haircut was a victory, a defeat and neither. It was a victory because Greece got more time and money, while securing its spot in the Eurozone. It was also a failure since the second bailout was needed only because the first had failed. But it was also neither a victory nor a defeat. As Aldous Huxley once wrote, "experience is not what happens to you. It is what you do with what happens to you." Despite this ambivalence, and the overall positive attitude towards the news, the country's political scene was shaken when Papandreou announced a referendum on the haircut. The referendum was surprising and unilateral, with politicians both in and out of Greece and PASOK being opposed to it. It was a also "rhetorical" referendum. It offered no real choice. The prime minister claimed that the people should approve the haircut to help the country "stave off default," a claim that was ludicrous since the haircut was the official stamp on default. The referendum felt like asking a vegetarian to pick between chicken and beef—yes, there is a choice, but it is irrelevant. This was another ultimatum to create the illusion of public support for policies that no one supported anymore. By November 2011, more than half the country thought it was time for elections.

Table 17—Public Opinion Metrics

Month	% Positive view of Papandreou	% Intend to Abstain	% Think Elections Needed
Oct-09	82%		
Nov-09	74%		
Dec-09	76%		
Jan-10	72%	15%	
Feb-10	72%	17%	
Mar-10	66%	23%	
Apr-10	68%	21%	
May-10	53%	34%	
Jun-10	53%	35%	
Jul-10	50%	36%	
Aug-10	50%		
Sep-10	50%	33%	
Oct-10	47%	33%	
Nov-10	43%	28%	
Dec-10	47%	29%	
Jan-11	44%	34%	14%
Feb-11	44%	34%	21%
Mar-11	35%	35%	22%
Apr-11	35%	36%	25%
May-11	34%	37%	22%
Jun-11	26%	38%	29%
Jul-11	28%	38%	37%
Aug-11	32%	35%	33%
Sep-11	30%	35%	31%
Oct-11	12%	34%	39%
Nov-11	19%	27%	54%
Dec-11	12%	33%	52%
Jan-12		33%	46%
Feb-12		29%	59%
Mar-12		23%	62%
Apr-12		19%	66%

Source: Public Issue, Political Barometers

Papandreou's resignation led to a weeklong scramble to agree on his successor as three parties came together to form a coalition (PASOK, New Democracy and the Popular Orthodox Rally, known as LAOS). On November 11, 2011, Lucas Papademos, a former governor of the Bank of Greece and vice president of the European Central Bank, became as Greece's 183rd prime minister. But his mandate was very limited: negotiate the haircut with the creditors, agree on the terms for the second bailout with the troika, and then hold national elections. Politics stopped. The desire for elections was getting so strong that the details of the second bailout package were not discussed at all. The new program, whose details the IMF released in March 2012, rested on the desire to: "(i) restore competitiveness and growth; (ii) restore fiscal sustainability; and (iii) secure financial stability." It would achieve these three goals through internal devaluation: "Resolving Greece's balance of payments problem within the euro will require a shift in the structural reform strategy to directly prioritize internal devaluation."[21] However, as the IMF, noted: "Restoring competitiveness by way of internal devaluation has proved to be a difficult undertaking with very few successes."[22] In fact, Box 3, a two-page section in the IMF report called "International Experience with Internal Devaluation" read as a perfect refutation of internal devaluation. And yet this was the pillar of the new program. It forecasted a prolonged contraction in private consumption, making the program harder to defend politically, and it made overly optimistic assumptions about exports and investment (at or above historical growth trends) to make the numbers add up. From the beginning, this was a tough sell. But it did no matter because no one was paying attention—everyone was focused on the elections.

The May and June 2012 Elections

In April, Papademos announced that elections would be held on May 6, 2012, and so the country entered, finally, an official campaign season. Then, on May 6, 2012, the Greek people finally got a chance to speak. No doubt, they renounced the status quo. But what they said, precisely, was hard to decipher. Good answers depend on good questions, and these elections were anything but a chance to ask good questions. What did the results show?

Table 18—Parliamentary Election Results

Party	Jun-12			May-12			Oct-09		
	%	Votes	Seats	%	Votes	Seats	%	Votes	Seats
New Democracy	29.66%	1,825,637	129	18.85%	1,192,051	108	33.47%	2,295,719	91
SYRIZA	26.89%	1,655,086	71	16.78%	1,061,282	52	4.60%	315,665	13
PASOK	12.28%	755,868	33	13.18%	833,527	41	43.92%	3,012,542	160
Independent Greeks	7.51%	462,466	20	10.61%	670,957	33			
Golden Dawn	6.92%	425,990	18	6.97%	441,018	21	0.29%	19,624	
Democratic Left	6.26%	385,077	17	6.11%	386,263	19			
Communist Party	4.50%	277,204	12	8.48%	536,072	26	7.54%	517,249	21
Recreate Greece/Action/Lib. Alliance	1.59%	98,061							
Popular Orthodox Rally	1.58%	97,094		2.90%	183,467		5.63%	386,205	15
Ecologist Greens	0.88%	54,420		2.93%	185,410		2.53%	173,589	
ANTARSYA	0.33%	20,391		1.19%	75,428		0.36%	24,687	
Democratic Alliance				2.56%	161,595				
Recreate Greece				2.15%	135,965				
Action - Liberal Alliance				1.80%	114,058				
Others	1.60%	98,371		5.49%	347,003		1.66%	113,141	
Totals	100%	6,155,665	300	100%	6,324,096	300	100%	6,858,421	300
Total votes (including invalids)		6,217,000			6,476,745			7,044,606	
Participation Rate		62.47%			65.10%			70.95%	

Source: Ministry of Interior. Table only shows parties that received over 1% of the vote in either of the 2012 elections. Parties need to receive 3% of the vote to enter parliament

First, the political system collapsed, reflecting the profound ambivalence of the Greek people. The first party (New Democracy) got less than 19% of the vote, while the top two got less than 36%. By contrast, in every election since 1981, the top two parties had gotten at least 77% of the vote and as much as 87%. PASOK received its lowest share of the popular vote ever (even below the 1974 elections when it was formed). Thirteen parties got more than 1%, while seven crossed the 3% threshold required to enter parliament (versus five in the 2009 election). Another two came close. A full 19% voted for parties that did not enter parliament, up from 5% in 2009. A fifth of the public was thus without any formal representation in parliament. The participation rate, at 65%, was below the 71% rate in 2009.[23]

Second, SYRIZA, a leftist coalition, registered a meteoric rise, receiving almost 17% of the vote, up from under 5% in 2009. Its electoral success was broad based: most of PASOK's 2009 voters who did not vote for PASOK voted for SYRIZA; the same was true for the Communist Party of Greece. SYRIZA, however, also attracted new constituencies: 30% of new voters and 19% of the people who did not vote in the 2009 elections voted for SYRIZA. It was also the party most favored by employees (public and private), the unemployed, and students—and its appeal was high for all but the oldest voters (aged 54+).[24] In effect, SYRIZA replaced PASOK and pushed the electorate to the left since its economic program, which was only seriously discussed after the election, showed a strong commitment to socialist ideas and ideals, supporting:

- The renationalization of all companies and organizations that have been "partly or fully privatized."
- The nationalization of "sectors that [are] critical to economic growth, such as ports, airports, roads, shipyards, mining and energy."
- The nationalization of banks to create a "reformed financial system based on banks with public ownership."
- The removal of "any [private] and [business] activity from education at all levels."
- The "shrinkage and eventual elimination of private sector participation in health" because there is "no room for profiteering" from health. This will be accomplished through the "universality and the quality of public sector care."
- The strength of labor rights: "Stable work conditions as enshrined in the constitution with life-long tenure in the public sector, in public enterprises, and in

banks, and through permanent contracts provide security to workers, reduce their reliance on political and
other pressure and make work more efficient."

- Ensure a state in which, "a guaranteed minimum income, a house with heating, lighting and telecommunications, food and clothing, transportation, help at
home, legal protection and representation are the right
of all citizens."

- Financing this state through a "radical overhaul of the
tax system, and the burdening, as much as needed, of
large incomes and accumulated wealth, coupled with
the reduction of spending that does not serve the
public interest." There is also a "different role for the
European Central Bank to finance either directly or
through European public banks national budgets and
EU public investment programs."[25]

Third, Golden Dawn, an ultranationalist party, got
6.97% of the vote. Its anti-immigrant rhetoric resonated
with "law and order" folk and with people who feel be-
sieged in ghettos where the writ of the state was absent.
Golden Dawn was the second largest recipient of new voters, but drew most of its electoral strength from the right
(former New Democracy and Popular Orthodox Rally voters). Fundamentally, this result reflected two truths: that the
country's immigration policy was unsustainable and that the
inability of the police to fight crime was creating demand for
extra-legal solutions. Long-term support for the party would
depend on the state's capacity to cater to these needs.

Fourth, four parties with liberal-reformist credentials
(Democratic Alliance, Recreate Greece, Liberal Alliance and
Action) collectively got ~6.5% of the vote. Since none surpassed the 3% threshold, their collective weight meant nothing electrically. However, these results showed a steady support for liberal reforms—keeping in mind that, for example,

the Communist Party of Greece has gotten around 4.5 to 8% of the vote since 1993. Given that these four parties suffered from a fear that a vote for these parties would be wasted (as it was since none got 3%), the true support for these parties' position was higher.

Fifth, there was a split between the urban and the rural vote. The major urban centers all went for leftist SYRIZA, while New Democracy carried almost all other areas (except Crete). No election since 1981 showed a similar decisive split between the major cities and the rest of the country. This underscored the difference in radicalism between the larger and the smaller cities and a hesitation outside the major urban centers to support a more radical leftist rhetoric. It could have also underscored the benefits of EU subsidies towards agriculture. It is no wonder that older voters (55 and above) voted for New Democracy above all other parties.

But with the collapse of the political system, the field remained wide-open to new politics, to new parties, and to new people. The old died but the new had yet to arrive. A full 19% of the people were courageous enough to gamble with their vote, showing a willingness to experiment and to try paths outside the establishment. Even more, the liberal parties got 6.5% of the vote—if people were not afraid that voting for them would mean a wasted vote, their share could have been higher, perhaps 9–10%.

The inability to form a government produced a second round of elections scheduled for June 17. These were the elections of consolidation. The Democratic Alliance (2.56% in the first round) joined with New Democracy, while the other three liberal-reformist parties merged as well. But otherwise, the electoral slate was just as wide as on May 6. Even so, the voters rallied: only 9 parties got over 1% of the vote (versus 13 in the May elections); the top two parties got 57%, still a historical low but much above the May vote of 36%; and the share of people who voted for parties that did not cross the threshold to get into parliament fell to a more normal 6% (versus 19% in the first election). Every party except New Democracy, SYRIZA, and the Democratic Left got a lower share of the vote in June than in May, evidence of the consolidation that happened. The groups that really elected New Democracy were pensioners, housewives, and the rural vote. That was the conservative rally, and it was mostly a reaction to the fear that a SYRIZA win would force Greece out of the Eurozone given SYRIZA's insistence to renegotiate the bailout with the troika. In the end, Greece got a coalition government formed by New Democracy, PASOK, and the Democratic Left party—fielding a collective 48% of the popular vote.

The back-to-back elections led to higher tensions and heightened rhetoric. But they also, soon after they were over, produced a renewed focus on the agenda that had effectively been stalled. For example, the coalition was soon consumed with identifying almost €12 billion in tax hikes and spending cuts—although these were known since the new loan package was signed in March 2012, there was no public debate about them. The other thing that happened was a marked change in tone. For much of the campaign season, the emphasis had shifted from what Greece can do for itself to what Europe can do for it. This changed after the election and there was an appreciation, for example, of how few of the provisions of the memorandum with the troika the Greek government had actually implemented.

The Political Economy of Failure

Greece and Papandreou were dealt a difficult hand in 2009. Reform to the extent that Greece needed is always hard to achieve, and the "the reformer who attempts to do everything all at once ends up accomplishing little or nothing."[26] Papandreou's problem was not his commitment to reforms (which was sincere) but his strategy for achieving them. As Huntington noted:

In theory two broad strategies are open to the reformer who desires to bring about a number of significant changes in social-economic structure and political institutions. One strategy would lead him to make known all his goals at an early time and to press for as many of them as he could in the hope of obtaining as much as possible. The alternative strategy is the foot-in-the-door approach of concealing his aims, separating the reforms from each other, and pushing for only one change at a time. The former is a comprehensive, "root," or blitzkrieg approach; the latter is an incremental, "branch," or Fabian approach. At various times in history reformers have essayed both methods. The results of their efforts suggest that for most countries subjected to the strains and dissentions involved in modernization, the most effective method of reform is the combination of a Fabian strategy with blitzkrieg tactics. To achieve his goals the reformer should separate and isolate one issue from another, but, having done this, he should, when the time is ripe, dispose of each issue as rapidly as possible, removing it from the political agenda before his opponents are able to mobilize their forces. The ability to achieve this proper mix of Fabianism and blitzkrieg is a good test of the political skill of a reformer.[27]

Papandreou pushed hard and passed enough reforms to alienate many of the constituencies that had brought PASOK to power and that formed its electoral backbone, but he did not push hard enough to win over the constituencies that would have benefited from change, nor did he articulate persuasively how the changes that he advocated would led to material improvements for people. His challenge was familiar and was one that Machiavelli had captured in *The Prince*:

There is nothing more difficult to carry out, nor more doubtful of success, nor more dangerous to handle, than to initiate a new order of things. For the reformer has enemies in all those profit by the old order, and only lukewarm defenders in all those who would profit by the new order, this lukewarmness arising partly from fear of their adversaries, who have laws in their favour; and partly from the incredulity of mankind, who do not truly believe in anything new until they have had actual experience of it. Thus it arises that on every opportunity for attacking the reformer, his opponents do so with the zeal of partisans, the others defend him half-heartedly, so that between them he runs great danger.[28]

But what exactly did Papandreou do and where did he go wrong? The path to reform would have to rest on four pillars: capacity, equity, ownership, and politics.

Capacity. Wanting to reform is not enough. To change, a state also needs administrative capacity, institutions and a national bureaucracy that can be deployed to serve a reform agenda. Greece's public administration was weak, meaning that the state bureaucracy could not conceive, legislate, coordinate, or implement change. Reform, as a result, was piecemeal, misguided, or unimplemented. A 2011 OECD report on Greece's public administration noted:

The apparent inability of successive Greek governments to implement measures that were enacted can be traced back to important weaknesses, which were allowed to persist in the functioning of the public administration. In particular, Greece's central administration was plagued with inefficient structures, inadequate access to information, and lack of co-ordination. Such problems had become a hallmark of the Greek government system long before the financial crisis, with considerable costs for the Greek economy and society.[29]

Greece faced an added problem. In order to reduce its deficit, the government was reducing the civil service. Of course, such a reduction was necessary, both to alleviate budgetary pressures as well as to lower redundancies. But this reduction was not tied to performance, and anecdotal evidence suggested that ministries were losing capable staff; as one staff member told me, "The people who left were the only ones working." So there was a tension between shrinking the bureaucracy, which was necessary, and retaining competent staff, which was not happening.

Equity. In a country with so many injustices and problems, sustaining political support reform rested on a sense of equity—that reform would affect everyone, not just the poor and the middle class. There was a tacit agreement that George Papaconstantinou, the finance minister, understood. Greeks, he said, would tolerate hardship as long as it was evenly distributed; if PASOK tried to insulate its own constituencies, public support would crumble. The debate to liberalize "closed professions" was a turning point in that regard because it was the first time that the government violated the (unspoken) pact that it had made with the electorate. The bill to liberalize the "closed professions" had too many loopholes and exemptions and set a long consultation period to define the ways in which the opening up would be limited to protect the public interest. The popular complaint against the government changed. In 2010, there was a fear that the government was moving too slowly, but at least its laws were making a difference and instituting reforms that the country needed. This law was the first evidence that the laws being passed no longer mattered. It is no wonder that the drop in the prime minister's popularity from February to March 2011 was the single largest one-month except the signing of the bailout itself and the announcement of a referendum that ultimately led to his resignation.

The government failed to apply equity in other ways. Jobs in the private sector declined by a much greater amount than jobs in the protected public sector where firing underperformers was almost impossible. Employees at state-owned enterprises were another privileged group, which seemed to earn average salaries that were unheard of in the private sector. And throughout 2010 and 2011, the government seemed to make little progress to tackle tax evasion or fight corruption. All these failures violated a sense of equity.

Ownership. In a scene in Romeo and Juliet, Apothecary says, "My poverty, but not my will, consents."[30] Greece felt similarly about the bailout. Despite the extent of the crisis, the country spent little time introspecting. Consider, for example, what the governor of the Bank of Greece wrote in the bank's 2010 Annual Report (published in April 2011):

> The causes of the crisis and the effort required have not been adequately explained to the public. The policy launched in May 2010 called into question certainties long considered unchallengeable and came up against entrenched attitudes. Nevertheless, there are still a number of questions that call for convincing answers: How did we get to where we stand today? Why did the growth model of the last 30 years collapse and what is the meaning of a "new growth model?" What is the real situation today? What rights, obligations, opportunities, possibilities, responsibilities and constraints does our participation in the EU and the euro area give rise to? What are the alternatives and what would they cost? What risks lie ahead and how can we address them? What will the final outcome of this effort be and, more importantly, how is it connected to the changes being promoted?[31]

The elites were either silent or apportioned blame widely—in effect, they said "everything went wrong." Collective blame found its most provocative expression in Theodoros Pangalos, who was a vice president in the cabinet of George Papandreou. Asked about "where the money went," he said, "We ate it all together." In some ways, he was right. And in other ways, he was wrong.

He was wrong for three reasons. First, not everyone cheated. Not everyone evaded taxes, built homes illegally, had a well-paying job in the public sector or received largesse from the state. Not every businessman was a thief or politician a fraud. Second, cheating is not binary. Cheating is bad, but more cheating is worse than less cheating. Equating the big cheats with the little ones is unfair. Third, by saying that everyone is to blame, no one is to blame. Everyone is responsible, no one is responsible. And yet he was right for one big reason. There is more to Greece's woes than stealing at the top. State spending rose in the 1980s but this money went to civil servants and to pensioners. Yes there was corruption, but it did not benefit fifty or a hundred people. It benefited thousands if not millions of people with connections who received public largesse and collected unearned benefits. Rich people evaded taxes but so did mom-and-pop shops—and sometimes the consumer who paid less for goods and services. Three-hundred billion euros is a lot of debt to pile up by stealing alone.

The problem is that broad a responsibility lets everyone off the hook, but narrow responsibility risks downplaying the insanities of contemporary Greece. Outrage for a million-euro bribe is easy; but what about a million euros paid to public sector employees who do not show up for work or to "blind" people who are not blind?[32] Can society be outraged with both? How to blame leaders but not the electorate? Yet how can millions be culpable for the actions of a few politicians? How can you blame a country for borrowing too much without blaming its lenders? One needs a partner to over-borrow. These are profound questions that defy easy answers.

What did the Greek people think? Public Issue conducted two polls asking respondents to identify how responsible they held a list of culprits for Greece's debt.[33] In decreasing culpability, they said: Greek governments, speculators, Greek banks, big EU states (e.g., Germany, France), foreign banks, Greek citizens, and Greece's into the Eurozone. Their responses showed ambivalence about the roots of the crisis.

Table 19—Greek Debt: How Responsible Do you Hold the Following? (% very)

Responsible Party	November 2010	May 2011
Greek governments	96%	98%
Speculators	87%	89%
Greek banks	72%	70%
Big EU states (e.g., Germany, France)	69%	67%
Foreign banks	66%	60%
Greek citizens	44%	52%
Entry into Euro & Eurozone	46%	44%

Source: Public Issue

That ambivalence persisted throughout, raising a deeper question: was Greece even a democracy? This was perhaps the most fundamental question. What does sovereignty mean and did the Greek people even have a choice about what happened to them? How could Greece be a democracy if all meaningful decisions were made by a handful of bureaucrats, mostly non-Greek and mostly non-elected?

In a narrow sense, of course, the Greek government remained sovereign. The various bailouts with the troika were negotiated by governments that retained parliamentary majorities and that survived votes of non-confidence in parliament. A number of elections—local or national—showed public support for the bailouts, whether tacit or explicit, limited or widespread. This was not a case of unelected officials bargaining away the country's future; these officials were put there, at one point or another, by the Greek people. Yet policymaking clearly shifted to a joint council that included the Ministry of Finance, the troika, and various other departments and agencies of the Greek government (depending on the subject). Wage cuts, pension reform, VAT increases, public sector accounting and accountability, privatizations, administrative simplification, the opening of closed professions, and the liberalization of product markets—in none of these was the Greek government alone in deciding what course to take. In fact, the government was an executor, not an architect. Even if one saw the memorandum as the act of a sovereign government, the changes that Greece was called to make went far beyond any considered during the October 2009 elections. No one voted for these changes in 2009.

Yet what is a democracy anyway? Interestingly, the Greek language makes no distinction between democracy and republic. If conceived narrowly, elected representatives governing based on the will of the people, then Greece failed the democracy test in many ways. But if democracy is conceived as something akin to a republic, then Greece became more democratic. Yes, the rights of truckers or seamen or lawyers or doctors or pharmacists were being curtailed—but should they have had those rights to begin with? What "right" is there to restrict competition and coerce the consumer to pay more? What "right" does the public sector employee have to get paid twice as much for half the work? These are not rights in any real sense—they are political abuses, perpetuated by politicians whose chief purpose is reelection for the sake of power and enrichment. Democracy means not just representative elections but checks and balances.

Yet this was a situation that continued to unsettle the Greek people. Two events captured the zeitgeist. First came the question, in early 2012, of whether Greece should accept a "budget commissioner" to supervise the budget and retain veto rights over fiscal matters. The suggestion angered the Greek political class and public at large. The idea was indeed a bad one, but not for the reasons that Greek politicians claimed.

Finance Minister Evangelos Venizelos said the proposal would force Greece to pick between "financial assistance" and "national dignity." Of course, national dignity is a relative term: when the country was seeking another €130 billion because it failed to implement the provisions of the first, €110 billion bailout; when the country was negotiating to cut over €100 billion in debt because it could no longer pretend to be able to repay it; when the country was derided daily in the international press; when its statistics were suspect and its promises empty; when all decisions were taken in tandem with foreign bureaucrats; and when the only momentum for meaningful reform came from those same bureaucrats—then perhaps Venizelos could have done well to explain what dignity he was trying to protect. Greece did not need a budget commission because at some point, its politicians should have stood up and taken ownership of the reform agenda. If Greece liberalized professions, collected taxes, privatized state-owned enterprises, modernized the state bureaucracy, and streamlined the functions of the state only because the troika said so, there was no hope. Greece needed to own this agenda. It needed people who will say that these things were worthwhile not because the troika said so but because they were the right thing to do. As long as Greek politicians said, "the troika made me do it" they demonstrated nothing more than their own inadequacy. The debate over the "commissioner" revealed the sustained lack of ownership over the reform agenda and the political class' tendency to eschew its own responsibilities by pointing the finger at the troika.

The second event was more subtle but no less important. During and around the May election, the national conversation changed. Introspection gave way to anger, and whatever reform momentum existed subsided in favor of a search for scapegoats. The relevant questions were no longer: "how can Greece change?" Instead, Greeks kept asking, "What does the victory of François Hollande in France mean," and "will Angela Merkel really kick Greece out of the Eurozone?" Greece's new motto was, ask not what you can do for your country; ask what Europe can do for you. This was a subtle change: after all, there has always been a keen interest in the international environment and how it affected Greece. But in mid-2012, Greece abandoned the internal debate. Greek society became obsessed with the "memorandum" and whether to repeal it, abrogate it, cancel it, amend it, renegotiate it, or change it. No discussions about privatizations, salaries, taxes, closed professions, and so on. Greece turned its eyes on Europe, treating this like a chess game, where gauging the move of the side is the most important thing. Except, of course, that this was a chess game on a sinking ship: Greece might have won the game, but who cares if the country ends up drowning in the end? In this process, Greece said: "This is all Europe's fault, we are but a victim. Help us." In the beginning of the crisis, Greeks understood that this crisis, while influenced by international events, had Greek characteristics. It exposed flaws in the way that Greek society and the Greek economy have been organized. To deal with the crisis, Greece had to cut spending, reform the public and private sector and upgrade the functionality of the state. Amidst the elections, this introspection was done. Much of Greece disowned the crisis, saying there was nothing it could do anymore. Greece changed from being a fat kid that was going on a diet to a fat kid that wants to sue the candy company. In the end, the fat kid may get a check, but will he get any thinner?

Politics. Was there political support for change? This question can be split into three: First, was there a social consensus on the broad direction that the country needed to take? Second, what form did social and political mobilization take and did it favor change? And third, did the political system believe it could achieve better electoral outcomes through reform?

There was clearly a consensus against the status quo, broadly understood: the high intention to abstain throughout 2011 and early 2012, coupled with the dissemination of the May 2012 vote are evidence enough that much of the electorate did not feel persuaded by any one program. A year after the bailout, Public Issue did a poll that reinforced the collapse of Greece's politico-economic model: 89% of respondents thought the country needed either radical change (56%) or a revolution (33%). Since 1999, there has been growing radicalization and those who thought minor changes were sufficient now thought a "revolution" is necessarily. Revolution, of course, is a vague term, and those most supporting revolution were the communists. But at least half of those who voted for the major parties (except the communists) thought "major change" was needed.[34]

No doubt people were against something, but were they for something also? One data point that suggested a desire for liberal reforms was the collapse in the prime minister's popularity during the closed professions debate. A poll conducted soon thereafter, in April 2011, reinforced that there was some consensus toward the direction of change. Consider the following responses:

- Around 58% of respondents had a favorable view of the private sector, while a mere 17% thought highly of the public sector.
- The share of people who had a negative reaction to the phrase "public sector" had grown from 35% to 59%.
- Around 58% of respondents said public sector employees should not have lifelong tenure. The share of those supporting tenure had fallen from 40% to 35% within a year.
- Around 74% thought privatizations are essential; only

21% doubt they were needed.

- Around 69% thought the country should strengthen the private sector to generate growth, up from 56% in 2006. A mere 11% thought growth should mainly come from the public sector and 15% thought the two were equally important.

- Support for privatizing state-owned companies had increased, with the most dramatic changes seen in railroads (65% said yes vs. 41% in 2008), Postal Savings (54% vs. 32%) and gaming company OPAP (60% vs. 46%). Support for privatizing the power company had also risen from 40% to 48%, but the public remained torn. Only for the National Bank of Greece was there a fall in the support for privatization.[35]

How about social mobilization? At first, the public's instinct was to acquiesce and to be patient. That is why there was so little protest through 2010. But then things changed. Who was protesting in Greece and why?

Broadly speaking, the frustration came from three corners. The first corner included the people who protested because they saw reforms as a threat to their privileges. The group consisted of public sector employees whose wages were threatened and whose ability to live off the public purse while offering (usually mediocre) services would be limited. But this group extended into the private sector as well. No one should think of Greece as having an inflated public sector and a productive private sector: distortions in the private sector are just as pervasive. Opposition to opening up professions was fierce, as evidenced by strikes among truckers, pharmacists, taxi drivers, and others. Even pensioners and others who received social benefits fall into this category, although the legitimacy of their grievances varies.

The second corner was harder to delineate but it consisted of two subgroups. It included first the perennial protestors. This group was more left than right and was unappeasable—its opposition ran deep and was as much ideological as practical. It protested in the name of anarchism or socialism, and its opposition was almost independent of who is in charge and what they were doing. Such opposition far predated the current crisis. These protestors were joined by a second sub-group, whose motives were vaguer. A deep sense of injustice from corruption was their most unifying rallying cry. Judging from opinion polls, however, this group had a diverse view of how Greece got into its mess. Besides corrupt politicians, it blamed speculators, banks, and other European governments for Greece's debt—much more so than Greek society, for example. By casting blame so widely, this group was casting blame nowhere at all. Its agenda was more "against" something rather than "for" something.

The third corner included people who believed reforms were too slow. This group was the most constructive force in Greek society—it was also the least represented in the "street." It was liberal, meritocratic, and opposed to clientelism. It was likely well educated, possibly with time spent abroad, and was younger rather than older. It saw Greek society as too constricting and the economy as offering too few opportunities. It struggled with whether to stay in Greece or leave. It saw momentum for change but it also saw politics hijacked by special interests and narrow-minded politicians. It wanted change but saw that change was not coming rapidly enough.

Of these three groups, who protested the most? One way to answer this question is to combine polls by Public Issue that set a participation rate by profession with information from tax returns, the Ministry of Finance, or the Hellenic Statistical Authority on the total size of the specific grouping. Around 55% of the protestors came from the private sector, either as employees (28%) or employers (27%), although the participation rate for the former was higher than the latter. Public sector employees protested the most

(57%), and they made up 17% of the total. Pensioners (13%), the unemployed (9%), and housewives (6%) made up the balance.

Very crudely, the protest was as much driven by self-interest (self-employed professionals, public sector employees, some pensioners) as by overall frustration. And yet, there was also hidden hope in that complete collapse of the system. Looking at protestors by political affiliation showed that almost a third of the protestors planned to abstain from elections. This was roughly in line with the overall intention to abstain, and it reinforced just how wide-open the political system became with a huge share of the electorate eager to rally behind a compelling platform.

Table 20—Greece: Estimated Protestors (May 2010-May 2011) by Employment

Profession / Status	Est. Total	Participation	# of Protestors	% Total	Source
Private Sector Employees	1,322,907	49%	648,224	28%	2
Self-employed	2,045,912	30%	613,774	27%	2
Public Sector Employees	705,645	57%	402,218	17%	1
Pensioners	2,100,000	14%	294,000	13%	3
Unemployed	680,200	29%	197,258	9%	3
Housewives	1,139,000	13%	148,070	6%	3
Total		37%	2,303,544	100%	

Sources: (1) Ministry of Finance. (2) Tax Returns. (3) Hellenic Statistical Authority. Protestor participation from Public Issue

The demand for reform, however, found no supply. In part, this was because PASOK remained split on the merits of reform. While Papandreou sincerely believed in the need for radical reform, he was never able to create a consensus in his cabinet in favor of that position. As a result, there were continuous battles, often in public, among ministers over the government's agenda. In part, this was mere politicking and it reflected the quest for power or the desire to curry favor with a constituency. But it was also due to ideology: getting a socialist party to overhaul a country's economy along market lines was a tough sell. It became especially tough as PASOK got caught in a vicious cycle where declining popularity led more party members to hedge their positions, which in turn stalled reforms that intensified public discontent and hence contributed to declining popularity. Soon PASOK got stuck in neutral: it was reforming enough to alienate and ultimately lose its traditional loyalists but it was not reforming enough to gain over the silent majority, which abandoned the prime minister in early 2011.

In the end, PASOK failed because it tried to do too much and it could not move on—it opened up new fights but rarely closed old ones. It thus faced a mobilization that was perpetually growing and never shrinking. It lost its base but won no one else.

EPILOGUE

Isaiah Berlin once wrote that, "Crucial turning points in history tend to occur, we are told, when a form of life and its institutions are increasingly felt to cramp and obstruct the most vigorous productive forces alive in a society—economic or social, artistic or intellectual—and it has not enough strength to resist them."[1] Greece struggled to find those "vigorous productive forces" in the first two years of the crisis. The country had rebellion in its DNA, but this rebellion was not of the productive type; after all, the birthmark of this crisis was the murder of three people who wanted to work while others went on strike. Caught in a cycle of economic contraction and political disappointment, Greece hit a nadir. By the middle of 2012, no one expected much of Greece anymore. Markets expected it neither to repay its debts nor stay in the Eurozone. Foreign officials doubted that Greece had either the will or the capacity to change; they merely begged for a faint gasp of reform—any reform. The investor had closed his checkbook, while the rapidly depleting bank balance had turned into a countdown to desperation for the middle class. The unemployed no longer expected to find a job, and the employed no longer expected to survive on whatever job they did have. The infirm had given up on health, the vulnerable on the "safety net," the parent on education, and the citizen on the police. Fighting tax evasion, selling state assets, reforming the public sector, opening up the private sector—in all, expectations were shrinking faster than the economy. Greece was at zero. Low expectations make it hard to turn a country around. People do what you expect of them: if you treat people as if they are unlikely to achieve much, they are unlikely to achieve much. As J. Sterling Livingston wrote in *Pygmalion in Management*: "The way managers treat their subordinates is subtly influenced by what they expect of them. If managers' expectations are high, productivity is likely to be excellent. If their expectations are low, productivity is likely to be poor. It is as though there were a law that caused subordinates' performance to rise or fall to meet managers' expectations."[2]

Yet there was also something refreshing about low expectations. As any underdog knows, exceeding expectations is easier when the expectations are low. Imagine what good news (genuine good news, not propaganda) could have done for Greece. Imagine if people believed that reforms were moving forward. Foreign governments would pledge more money and give Greece more time. Investors would sign up for more short-term Greek debt, perhaps even medium and long-term debt. If the Greek people believed in their government and were willing to allocate a share of their savings to finance state spending, the country's financing needs would be more easily covered. Investment—foreign and domestic—would rejuvenate the economy and yield revenue to the treasury. And the mental health of the Greek people would rebound from a belief that this endless descent into misery was coming to an end. Good news can do a lot. But how? Was this a lost cause from the beginning? In pondering this question, I have been drawn to a Walter Isaacson article called "The Real Leadership Lessons of Steve Jobs."[3] Based on Isaacson's biography of Steve Jobs, it distills what one could learn from the founder of Apple and one of the greatest business personalities of our times. The article has 14 lessons, but I think five will suffice.

Focus. "Deciding what not to do is as important as deciding what to do," Jobs said, and this is a lesson that most leaders will echo. It is easy for the Greek government to find one hundred things that need urgent fixing. And they are all important politically, economically, ethically, socially. Yet no person and no organization can fix a hundred things at once. And rather than trying, the government would be better served to focus on a few big things. My list would be tax evasion, judicial reform, entrepreneurship, physical security, and accountability in the public sector. These are big, broad tasks, of course. But how closer would Greece be in achieving them if it had devoted 90% of its resources to these five goals rather than allocating 5% each to 20 goals? Focus means discipline and it means learning to avoid distractions. It is hard work, but it means asking every day, "What did I do today to achieve these goals?"

Simplify. Together with "focus" comes "simplify." Simplicity, Jobs understood, came from "conquering, rather than merely ignoring, complexity." Anyone who has interacted with the Greek system knows its immense complexity. No task, however mundane, is truly simple (passport issuance is a rare exception). Simplicity requires a return to first principles, to look at each thing and ask, "What purpose does this serve?" and, "Do we really need it?" Imagine a serious commitment to simplicity, where the bureaucracy is pushed to ask, "How can I make this task simpler?" Imagine a place where simplification is rewarded by promotion and by pay. What would the Greek system look like then?

Put products before profits. Jobs said, "My passion has been to build an enduring company where people were motivated to make great products. Everything else was secondary. Sure, it was great to make a profit, because that was what allowed you to make great products. But the products, not the profits, were the motivation." Greece is not in the profit-making business. But Jobs understood that if you focus merely on profits you are no longer focusing on great products. Often, Greece seemed engaged in an effort to create elegant "five-year" plans. Pore over the numbers too long and you are missing the point of what governing is about. The goal is not to produce a piece of paper, but to change the country—if the country were to change, the debt math, the GDP math, the competitiveness math, they would all look better. A country, like a company, needs its priorities straight.

Don't be slaves to focus groups. Jobs liked to quote Henry Ford, who said, "If I'd asked customers what they wanted, they would have told me, 'A faster horse!'" Or, as Bill Cosby said: "I don't know the key to success, but the key to failure is trying to please everybody." In politics, it is hard to ignore constituencies. But with over a million unemployed, with pensioners and workers seeing their incomes shrink, with the extreme left and the extreme right gaining ground, and with such desperation and frustration, it is hard to see how reforms are "bad politics." Listening to what people want is important but only to a point. There is no way to get out of this crisis while making everyone happy—and in fact, the past few years have shown this to be true. Focus on the big picture not on every constituency.

When behind, leapfrog. When Apple missed the boat on music, "instead of merely catching up by upgrading the iMac's CD drive, [Jobs] decided to create an integrated system that would transform the music industry. The result was the combination of iTunes, the iTunes Store, and the iPod, which allowed users to buy, share, manage, store, and play music better than they could with any other devices." But what does it mean for Greece to leapfrog? Greece is trying to catch up. It is trying to adapt, to adopt "best practices," to close the gap. In some ways that is necessary. But crises are times for bold ideas. Countries have often leapfrogged with innovations such as flat taxes, special economic zones, or industrial clusters. What does leapfrog mean in tourism or shipping? How can the state help turn Piraeus into the premier shipping hub in the world, where ship owners, char-

terers, insurance companies, lawyers, and universities gather
to shape the future of the shipping industry? Why is that
beyond the capacity of the Greek state? In what other ways
can Greece leapfrog? No one achieved greatness by merely
copying others.

▪▪ ▪

What permeated the Jobs philosophy more fundamentally
was a commitment to excellence, a belief that doing great
things attracts first-rate people, challenges the human mind,
and fulfills the human spirit. When asked whether he was
rough on people, he said, "Look at the results ... These are
all smart people I work with, and any of them could get a
top job at another place if they were truly feeling brutalized.
But they don't ... And we got some amazing things done."
What Jobs brought was a sense of common purpose, a
shared journey to a great destination. And he built a great
brand.

What is Greece's brand? At its purest, most attractive
and most seductive, it is a country that can offer an unparal-
leled work-life balance. Life in Greece can be very good: the
problem in the "work-life balance" is "work." Ask any
Greek outside of Greece: If I could offer you the same job
and opportunities in Greece, would you move? An overwhelming majority would say yes. With a good job, Greece
offers an unbeatable work-life balance—its lifestyle is simply
too attractive to match almost anywhere in the world. Reha-
bilitating the Greek brand would mean "a place where you
can work hard and enjoy the fruits of your labor with a great
life." Or, more simply: "Work. Life. Balance."

What Greece needs is someone to believe in its potential for greatness again and in that brand. It needs a politician who believes that this country can be, as it was a few
decades ago, one of the most dynamic and fastest growing
in the developed world; who believes that Greece can offer
an unmatched tourist product that blends natural beauty,

history, and modernity; who believes that Greece can be a center for global shipping where young professionals come to build their careers and get ahead; who believes that Greece can be a magnet not merely for refugees and economic migrants but for skilled professionals and for Greeks who no longer feel they need to cross borders and oceans to find opportunities; who believes we can do great things together by getting the little things right—little things like rewarding good work and balancing our rights with our responsibilities to one another. This is a paradigm shift and it is what Greece needs not merely to lift itself up, but also to believe that there is something worth lifting itself up for. The expectations are so low that it does not take much to get people thinking differently both in and out of the country. If the crisis yields such leadership and hope, then it could turn into a blessing for all those who crave for a new and different Greece.

BIBLIOGRAPHY

Primary Sources, Reports, and Databases

Bank of Greece.

Bank of International Settlements.

ELSTAT (Hellenic Statistical Authority), *Statistical Yearbook of Greece*, *Statistical Bulletin of Public Finance*, *Building Activity Statistics*, Online databases.

European Central Bank.

European Commission, Reports on the Greek Program, Annual macro-economic database (AMECO).

EU Privatization Barometer.

EUROSTAT (Statistical Office of the European Communities).

Heritage Foundation / Wall Street Journal Economic Freedom index.

International Monetary Fund, Reports on Greek and other programs, World Economic Outlook (WEO) databases.

NATO, "Financial and Economic Data Relating to NATO Defense."

Ministry of Finance, National Budgets, Public Debt Bulletins, Budget Execution Bulletins.

OECD, *Economic Surveys of Greece*, Online databases.

Public Issue (public opinion company in Greece).

Transparency International, *Corruption Perception Index*.

World Bank, World Development Indicators and *Doing Business Report*.

World Economic Forum's *Global Competitiveness Report*.

United National Conference on Trade and Development (UNCTAD), Foreign direct investment database.

United Nations World Tourism Organization.

United States Census Bureau, *Lifetime Mobility in the United States 2010*. American Community Survey Briefs (ACSBR/10-07), November 2011.

Books, Articles, and Working Papers

Alfaro, Laura, Vinati Dev and Stephen McIntyre, "Foreign Direct Investment and Ireland's Tiger Economy," Harvard Business School, 9-706-007, Revised November 20, 2006.

Anholt, Simon. *Places: Identity, Image and Reputation.* New York: Palgrave Macmillan, 2010.

Artavanis, et. al., "Tax Evasion Across Industries: Soft Credit Evidence from Greece," Chicago Booth Paper No. 12–25, June 25, 2012.

Ash, Timothy Garton. "The Crisis of Europe." *Foreign Affairs*, September/October 2012.

Åslund, Anders. "Why Toomas Ilves Is Right and Paul Krugman Is Wrong," *Postimees* (Estonia), June 10, 2012.

Åslund, Anders. "Why a Collapse of the Euro Area Must Be Avoided, *VoxEU.org*, August 21, 2012.

Åslund, Anders. "Why a Breakup of the Euro Area Must Be Avoided: Lessons from Previous Breakups," Peterson Institute for International Economics Policy Brief 12-20, August 2012.

Åslund, Anders and Valdis Dombrovskis. *How Latvia Came through the Financial Crisis*, Washington, DC: Peterson Institute for International Economics, 2011.

Bauer, Peter. *From Subsistence to Exchange and Other Essays.* Princeton, NJ: Princeton University Press, 2000.

Bergsten, C. Fred. "Why the Euro Will Survive," *Foreign Affairs*, September/October 2012.

Berlin, Isaiah. "Fathers and Children." In *Russian Thinkers.* New York: Penguin Books, 1994.

Blanchard, O. and Francesco Giavazzi. "Current Account Deficits in the Euro Area. The End of the Feldstein-Horioka Puzzle?" *Brookings Papers on Economic Activity*, 2002:2.

Creswell, Julie and Graham Bowley, "Ratings Firms Misread Signs of Greek Woes," *The New York Times*, 29 November 2011.

Clogg, Richard. *A Concise History of Greece*. Cambridge: Cambridge University Press, 1992.

Clogg, Richard. *Parties and Elections in Greece*. London: C. Hurst & Company, 1987.

Clogg, Richard and George Yannopoulos, eds. *Greece under military rule*. New York: Basic Books, 1972.

Feldstein, Martin. "EMU and International Conflict," *Foreign Affairs*, November/December 1997.

Feldstein, Martin and Charles Horioka, "Domestic Saving and International Capital Flows." *Economic Journal* 358, 1980.

Freier, Maximilian "Political Economy of the Agenda 2010 Reforms: How Gerhard Schröder Overcame the 'Blocked Republic'," American Consortium on European Union Studies (ACES) EU Center of Excellence Washington, D.C., Cases No. 2008.3.

Friedman, Milton and Robert Mundell. "One World, One Money?" *Policy Options*, May 2001.

Frieden, Jeffry. "The Euro: Who Wins? Who Loses?" *Foreign Policy* 112 (September) 1998.

Friedman, Benjamin M. *The Moral Consequences of Economic Growth*. New York: Vintage, 2005.

Friedman, Milton. *Capitalism and Freedom*. Chicago: Chicago University Press, 1982.

Huntington, Samuel. *Political Order in Changing Societies*. New Haven: Yale University Press, 1968.

Iatrides, John O and Linda Wrigley, eds. *Greece at the Crossroads: The Civil War and Its Legacy*. University Park: Penn State Press, 1995.

International Monetary Fund (IMF), *World Economic Outlook: Recovery, Risk, and Rebalancing.* Washington, DC: International Monetary Fund, October 2010.

Isaacson, Walter. "The Real Leadership Lessons of Steve Jobs." *Harvard Business Review*, April 2012.

Karamanlis. *Poltical Speech.* Athens: Institute of Democracy: Constantine Karamanlis, 2004.

Kariotis, Theodore C. ed. *The Greek Socialist Experiment: Papandreou's Greece 1981–1989.* New York: Pella Publishing Company, 1992.

Kennedy, David M. *Freedom from Fear: The American People in Depression and War, 1929-1945.* Oxford: Oxford University Press, 1999.

Kentikelenis, et. al., "Health effects of financial crisis: omens of a Greek tragedy." *Lancet Online*, October 10, 2011.

Kindleberger, Charles. *Manias, Panics and Crashes*, 4th Edition. New York: Wiley Investment Classics, 2001.

Koliopoulos, J. and Thanos Veremis. *Greece: The Modern Sequel. From 1831 to Present.* New York: New York University Press, 2002.

Krugman, Paul. "Greece as Victim," *New York Times*, June 17, 2012.

Lewis, Michael. "Beware of Greeks Bearing Bonds." *Vanity Fair*, October 2010.

Livingston, Sterling. "Pygmalion in Management." *Harvard Business Review*, September–October 1988, Reprint 88509.

Malcolm, Noel. "The Case Against 'Europe'." *Foreign Affairs*, March/April 1995.

Merler, Silvia and Jean Pisani-Ferry. "The Simple Macroeconomics of North and South in EMU." Bruegel Working Paper 2012/12, July 2012.

Miller, James Edward. *The United States and the Making of Modern Greece: History and Power, 1950–1974.* Chapel Hill: The University of North Carolina Press, 2009.

Mundell, Robert A. "A Theory of Optimum Currency

Areas," *The American Economic Review*, Volume 51, Issue 4, September 1961.

Negreponti-Delivanis, M. *Greece in transition 1821-1971: Economic aspects*. Salonika: University of Salonika, 1979.

Orwell, George. Essays. New York: Everyman's Library, 2002.

Pew Research Center, "Pervasive Gloom About the World Economy," Global Attitudes Project Thursday, July 12, 2012.

Pisani-Ferry, Jean. "The Euro Crisis and the New Impossible Trinity," *Moneda y Credito* 234/2012.

Reinhart, Carmen M. and Kenneth Roggoff. 2009. *This Time is Different: Eight Centuries of Financial Folly*. Princeton: Princeton University Press, 2009.

Riegert, Bernd, "Crisis topples governments like dominos," *Deutsche Welle*. April 24, 2012.

Rogoff, Kenneth. "A euro parable: the couple with a joint account," *Financial Times*, April 23, 2012.

Roubini, Nouriel. "Greece's Best Option is an Orderly Default," *Financial Times*, June 28, 2010

Schneider, Friedrich, "Size and Development of the Shadow Economy of 31 European Countries from 2003 to 2010," September 2010.

Simitis, Kostas. *The Crisis* (I Krisi). Athens: Polis, 2008.

Squires, Nick. "Greek 'island of the blind'? More like 'island of welfare cheats'," *Christian Science Monitor*, April 30, 2012.

Veremis, Thanos. *The Military in Greek Politics*. New York: Black Rose Books, 1997.

Walker, Marcus. "Three Deaths Shifted Course of Greek Crisis," *Wall Street Journal*, November 27, 2010.

Waysand C., K. Ross and J. de Guzman, "European financial linkages: A new look at imbalances," *IMF Working Paper 10/295*, December 2010.

Weisbrot, Mark. "Why Greece Should Reject the Euro," *The New York Times*, May 10, 2011.

NOTES

Introduction
[1] IMF, "Staff Report on Request for Stand-By Arrangement," 28.

[2] Eurostat, "Government finance statistics," accessed November 9, 2012.

[3] Bank of Greece, "Government benchmark bond prices and yields," accessed November 9, 2012.

[4] Walker, "Three Deaths Shifted Course of Greek Crisis."

[5] Walker, "Three Deaths Shifted Course of Greek Crisis."

[6] IMF, "First Review Under the Stand-By Arrangement," 4—5.

[7] IMF, "Second Review Under the Stand-By Arrangement," 1.

[8] IMF, "Second Review Under the Stand-By Arrangement," 20—21.

[9] IMF, "Fourth Review Under the Stand-By Arrangement," 33.

[10] Council of Europe, "Statement by the Heads of State or Government of the Euro Area," 21 July 2011.

[11] ELSTAT, "04. Quarterly GDP - Expenditure Approach (Constant Prices)," accessed November 9, 2012.

[12] Bank of Greece, "Deposits held with credit institutions, breakdown by sector," accessed November 9, 2012.

[13] ELSTAT, "Labour force (Quarterly) - Timeseries," ac-

cessed November 9, 2012.

14 ELSTAT, "Labour force (Quarterly) - Timeseries," accessed November 9, 2012. ECB, "Greece - Compensation Per Employee, Current prices, National currency, Neither seasonally nor working day adjusted, Index," accessed November 9, 2012.

15 Kentikelenis, et. al., "Health effects of financial crisis: omens of a Greek tragedy."

16 Krugman, *Greece as Victim.*

17 Yanis Varoufakis, "Greek Crisis: Why There Is No Such Thing (And How To Escape It)," Lecture series in Melbourne, October 2012.

18 Roubini, "Greece's Best Option is an Orderly Default."

19 AMECO, "General government consolidated gross debt :- Excessive deficit procedure (based on ESA 1995) and former definition (linked series)," May 2012 update.

20 The conservatives won successive elections in June 1989, November 1989 and April 1990—but as the short duration between them suggests, there were run-off elections in search of a stable parliamentary majority.

21 In Orwell, *Essays*, 107.

What Happened in Greece?

1 M. Negreponti-Delivanis, *Greece in transition 1821-1971*, 138.

2 WDI, GDP per capita (current US$), accessed November 2, 2012.

3 WDI, Rural population (% of total population), accessed November 2, 2012.

4 ELSTAT, *Statistical Yearbook of Greece 1955*, p. 53.

5 OECD, *Economic Survey of Greece 1962*, 6.

6 WDI, Mortality rate, infant (per 1,000 live births), accessed November 2, 2012.

[7] WDI, Life expectancy at birth, total (years), accessed November 2, 2012.

[8] WDI, Telephone lines (per 100 people), accessed November 2, 2012.

[9] WDI, Food exports (% of merchandise exports), accessed November 2, 2012.

[10] OECD, *Economic Survey of Greece 1963*, 9—13.

[11] OECD, *Economic Survey of Greece 1979*, 35.

[12] OECD, *Economic Survey of Greece 1964*, 33

[13] WDI, "GDP growth (annual %)," accessed November 2, 2012.

[14] AMECO, "02 Gross national income per head of population," May 2012 update.

[15] OECD, *Economic Survey of Greece 1982*, 11.

[16] OECD, Economic Survey of Greece, 35.

[17] ELSTAT, Household expenditure survey 1981-1982, p. 19.

[18] ELSTAT, *Statistical Yearbook of Greece 1985*, pp.17—18; ELSTAT, *Social Welfare and Health Statistics 1981*, p. 21.

[19] WDI, "Crop production index (2004-2006 = 100)" and "Livestock production index (2004-2006 = 100)," accessed November 5, 2012.

[20] WDI, "Agricultural machinery, tractors per 100 sq. km of arable land," accessed November 2, 2012.

[21] ELSTAT, *National Accounts 1958—1975*, 13—14.

[22] ELSTAT, *National Accounts 1958—1975*, 13.

[23] ELSTAT, *National Accounts 1958—1975*, 13.

[24] OECD, *Economic Survey of Greece 1971*, 67; OECD, *Economic Survey of Greece 1987*, 63.

[25] AMECO Database, "Industrial production: construction excluded," May 2012 update.

[26] ELSTAT, *National Accounts 1958—1975*, 38.

[27] ELSTAT, *National Accounts 1958—1975*, 16.

[28] OECD, *Census of industry, crafts and commerce enterprises of 15 November 1958*, xxx.

[29] OECD, *Economic Survey of Greece 1972*, 37.

[30] OECD, *Economic Survey of Greece 1977*, 15.

[31] ELSTAT, *Industrial survey for the year 1980*, 12.

[32] OECD, *Economic Survey of Greece 1962*, 19.

[33] OECD, *Economic Survey of Greece 1978*, 35.

[34] "The expansion of industrial activity was, moreover, facilitated by the substantial increase in bank credit. Current credits to industry in fact represented in 1960 63 per cent of the gross value added of industrial production, compared with 38 per cent in 1955." OECD, *Economic Survey of Greece 1962*, 14.

[35] "Up to 1957, the State had practically no means of covering the deficit other than Central Bank lending and foreign aid. In 1958–60, however, the State was able to cover a large fraction of the overall deficit (about 47 per cent) by having direct recourse to internal savings, either by selling Treasury bonds to the banks or by issuing a long-term loan." OECD, *Economic Survey of Greece 1962*, 24.

[36] WDI, "Official exchange rate (LCU per US$, period average)," accessed November 2, 2012.

[37] ELSTAT, *National Accounts 1958—1975*, 35; OECD, Economic Survey of Greece 1984, 21.

[38] NATO, "Financial and Economic Data Relating to NATO Defense," various editions.

[39] OECD, *Economic Surveys*, various editions.

[40] ELSTAT, *National Accounts 1958—1975*, 34.

[41] ELSTAT, *Public Finance Statistics*, various editions.

[42] OECD, Economic Survey of Greece 1972, 24.

[43] ELSTAT, *Building Activity Statistics 1990* and *2008*; OECD, *Economic Survey of Greece 1975*, 9—10.

[44] OECD, *Economic Survey of Greece 1978*, 32; ELSTAT, *Statis-*

tical Yearbook of Greece 1981, 51.

[45] The 1960 number from OECD, Economic Survey of Greece 1979, 44; the 1980 number from ELSTAT, *Statistical Yearbook of Greece 1983*, 351.

[46] ELSTAT, *Statistical Yearbook of Greece 1962*, 301; ELSTAT, *Statistical Yearbook of Greece 1982, 384.*

[47] ELSTAT, *Statistical Yearbook of Greece 1962*, 300 and ELSTAT, *Statistical Yearbook of Greece 1981*, 390.

[48] OECD, *Economic Survey of Greece 1972*, 39—40; OECD, *Economic Survey of Greece 1978*, 33.

[49] OECD, *Economic Survey of Greece 1971*, 58.

[50] OECD, *Economic Survey of Greece 1973*, 33.

[51] OECD, *Economic Survey of Greece 1978*, 32—33.

[52] UNCTAD, Foreign Direct Investment Database, accessed 5 November 2012.

[53] Huntington, *Political Order in Changing Societies*, 5.

[54] Wikipedia, "List of Prime Ministers of Greece," accessed, November 15, 2012.

[55] Data from Clogg, *Parties and Elections in Greece.*

[56] Quoted in Clogg, *Parties and Elections in Greece,* 3—4.

[57] Karamanlis, Political Speech, 34—35.

[58] Iatrides, Greece at the Crossroads 1944—1950, 5.

[59] Clogg, *Concise History of Greece*, 117.

[60] Clogg, *Concise History of Greece*, 120.

[61] Iatrides, Greece at the Crossroads 1944—1950, 19.

[62] Iatrides, Greece at the Crossroads 1944—1950, 20.

[63] Clogg, *Concise History of Greece*, 125.

[64] Clogg, *Concise History of Greece*, 125.

[65] Iatrides, Greece at the Crossroads 1944—1950, 15.

[66] Iatrides, Greece at the Crossroads 1944—1950, 13.

[67] Iatrides, Greece at the Crossroads 1944—1950, 9.

[68] Iatrides, Greece at the Crossroads 1944—1950, 9.

[69] Iatrides, Greece at the Crossroads 1944—1950, 10.

[70] Iatrides, Greece at the Crossroads 1944—1950, 15—17.

[71] Clogg, *Concise History of Greece*, 147—148.

[72] In Kariotis, *The Greek Socialist Experiment*, 50.

[73] Clogg, *Concise History of Greece*, 157.

[74] Clogg, *Parties and Elections in Greece*, 48.

[75] Miller, *The United States and the Making of Modern Greece*, 26.

[76] Clogg, *Parties and Elections in Greece*, 26.

[77] Veremis, *The Military in Greek Politics*, 152.

[78] Miller, *The United States and the Making of Modern Greece*, 77.

[79] Miller, *The United States and the Making of Modern Greece*, 81.

[80] Miller, *The United States and the Making of Modern Greece*, 133.

[81] Miller, *The United States and the Making of Modern Greece*, 26.

[82] Miller, *The United States and the Making of Modern Greece*, 27.

[83] Miller, *The United States and the Making of Modern Greece*, 33.

[84] Miller, *The United States and the Making of Modern Greece*, 35—36.

[85] Miller, *The United States and the Making of Modern Greece*, 41.

[86] Miller, *The United States and the Making of Modern Greece*, 67.

[87] Miller, *The United States and the Making of Modern Greece*, 90.

[88] Clogg, *Concise History of Greece*, 23.

[89] Miller, *The United States and the Making of Modern Greece*, 28.

[90] Miller, *The United States and the Making of Modern Greece*, 34.

[91] Miller, *The United States and the Making of Modern Greece*, 73.

[92] Miller, *The United States and the Making of Modern Greece*, 136.

[93] Miller, *The United States and the Making of Modern Greece*, 154.

[94] Miller, *The United States and the Making of Modern Greece*, 207.

[95] In Kariotis, *The Greek Socialist Experiment*, 40.

[96] In Kariotis, *The Greek Socialist Experiment*, 46.

[97] In Kariotis, *The Greek Socialist Experiment*, 17.

[98] In Kariotis, *The Greek Socialist Experiment*, 54.

[99] OECD, *Economic Survey of Greece 1991*, 11.

[100] OECD, *Economic Survey of Greece 2001*, 50.

[101] ELSTAT, *Register of public services, corporate bodies of public law and state corporate bodies of private law 1998*, 7; ELSTAT, *Statistics on placements and dismissals or retirement of public servants for the year 1963*, 3

[102] ELSTAT, *Public Finance Statistics 1980—1981*, 22; ELSTAT, *Public Finance Statistics 1991*, 24; ELSTAT, *Statistical Yearbook of Greece 1983*, 439; ELSTAT, *Statistical Yearbook of Greece 1992—1993*, 496

[103] "The [law's] major defects were: first, the abolition of the general directors (permanent civil servants) at the top of the civil service hierarchy and their replacement by political appointees as 'special secretaries' and a multitude of 'counsellors'; second, the participation of all personnel from the different administrative units or from the politicised labour union cells in the 'councils' responsible for appointments to supervisory posts (e.g. directors, heads of sections), thus making the incumbents subject to pressure; third, the decoupling of pay and promotion from functions and responsibilities; and fourth, the great weight in recruitment given to the so-called 'social' criteria (number of children, family income, preference for people coming from distant regions, etc.). Furthermore, a cap was put on high salaries in the civil service, causing a fall in the after tax wage ratio between high and low categories to barely 2, irrespective of age and seniority, from almost 5 at the end of the 1970s40. This has demotivated senior personnel and young educated recruits aspiring to make a career in the civil service, and has also led to a severe shortage of professional and trained personnel." OECD, *Economic Survey 1992*, 58.

[104] OECD, *Economic Survey of Greece 1998*, 93.

[105] OECD, *Economic Survey of Greece 1987*, 47.

[106] For estimates of the number of people working in public enterprises, see OECD, *Economic Survey of Greece 2001*, 52. For the compensation ratio in 1997, see OECD, *Economic Survey of Greece 1998*, 106. For the ratio in 2008, see Ministry of Finance, "Oikonomika Apotelesmata 11 DEKO, 2007-2009," October 13, 2010.

[107] ELSTAT, *Statistics of transports and communication*, various editions.

[108] ELSTAT, *Statistics of transports and communications*, various editions.

[109] ELSTAT, *Statistics of transports and communications*, various editions.

[110] ELSTAT, *Statistics of transports and communications*, various editions.

[111] ELSTAT, *Statistics of transports and communications 1989—1991*, 81—84, and ELSTAT, *Statistics of transports and communications 1981*, 60—64.

[112] OECD, *Economic Survey of Greece 1998*, 96.

[113] OECD, *Economic Survey of Greece 1998*, 152.

[114] OECD, *Economic Survey of Greece 2003*, 171.

[115] OECD Statistics, "Social Expenditure: Public expenditure on old-age and survivors cash benefits, in % GDP," accessed November 3, 2012.

[116] OECD, *Economic Survey of Greece 1982*, 66.

[117] OECD, "Social Expenditure: Public expenditure on old-age and survivors cash benefits, in % GDP," accessed November 3, 2012. ELSTAT, *Statistical Yearbook of Greece 1983*, 96.

[118] ELSTAT, *Statistical Yearbook of Greece*, various editions.

[119] OECD, *Economic Survey of Greece 1996*, 82.

[120] ELSTAT, *Public Finance Statistics*, various editions.

[121] In Kariotis, *The Greek Socialist Experiment*, 243.

[122] For 1980 figure, see OECD, *Economic Survey of Greece 1990*, 124; for 1990 figure, see OECD, *Economic Survey of Greece 1992*, 105.

[123] OECD, *Economic Survey of Greece 1991*, 19.

[124] OECD, *Economic Survey of Greece 1991*, 17

[125] In 1955–1957, direct taxes were 3.5% of GDP in Greece versus 9.7% in OECD Europe; by 1974–1977, the ratio was 4.7% versus 14.6% in Europe. OECD, *Economic Survey of Greece 1979*, 34.

[126] In Kariotis, *The Greek Socialist Experiment*, 217.

[127] In Kariotis, *The Greek Socialist Experiment*, 254.

[128] OECD, *Economic Survey of Greece 1986*, 39.

[129] Miller, *The United States and the Making of Modern Greece*, p. 32.

[130] OECD, *Economic Survey of Greece 1991*, 14.

[131] OECD, *Economic Survey of Greece 1987*, 30.

[132] OECD, Economic Survey of Greece 1987, 30.

[133] "The increase in financial charges contributed almost two-fifths to the swing from net profits in 1979 to net losses in 1984 … In 1984 the net losses of the 3113 manufacturing firms surveyed amounted to Dr 38.5 billion, equivalent to a negative net profit rate of 13.6 per cent" OECD, *Economic Survey of Greece 1987*, 32—33.

[134] OECD, *Economic Survey of Greece 1991*, 18.

[135] ELSTAT, *Statistical Yearbook 1989*, 419.

[136] ELSTAT, *Statistical Yearbook*, sections "Tourist Movement—Hotel Units" and "Balance of Payments," various.

[137] OECD, *Economic Survey of Greece 1984*, 48.

[138] OECD, *Economic Survey of Greece 1987*, 38.

[139] OECD, *Economic Survey of Greece 1992*, 56.

[140] OECD, *Economic Survey of Greece 1993*, 31.

[141] OECD, *Economic Survey of Greece 1993*, 34.

[142] OECD, *Economic Survey of Greece 1992*, 11

143 The increase came from all sources, although direct taxes contributed the most (39% of the rise). AMECO, "16 Total revenue: general government :- ESA 1995," May 2012 update.

144 OECD, Economic Survey of Greece 1996, 141.

145 Eurostat, "Government finance statistics."

146 OECD, *Economic Survey of Greece 1993*, 83.

147 OECD, *Economic Survey of Greece 1993*, 83.

148 OECD, *Economic Survey of Greece 1998*, 111.

149 EU Privatization Barometer.

150 EU fund data from "Co financed Development Programmes," http://www.hellaskps.gr/1986-1999.htm. To calculate the share of total investment, I used the gross fixed capital formation numbers from AMECO's time series and the Greek GDP deflator.

151 ELSTAT, *Statistical Yearbook* , various editions.

152 Embassy of Greece, "Cost of Athens 2004 Olympics," Press Release, November 13, 2004.

153 European Commission, "Report on Greek Government Deficit and Debt Statistics," January 2010.

154 Eurostat, "Government bond yields, 10 years' maturity - annual data [irt_lt_gby10_a]," updated July 23, 2012.

155 ECB, "Harmonised long-term interest rates for convergence assessment purposes," accessed November 3, 2012.

Greece's Options—and Europe's

1 IMF, "Greece: Staff Report on Request for Stand-By Arrangement," 1.

2 Krugman, "Greece as Victim."

3 OECD, Government at a Glance 2011.

4 OECD, Economic Survey of Greece 2011, 91.

5 Ministry of Finance, "Oikonomika Apotelesmata 11 DEKO, 2007-2009," October 13, 2010.

[6] OECD, Government at a Glance 2011.

[7] OECD, Economic Survey of Greece 2009, 88.

[8] OECD, "Health Data 2012."

[9] Based on OECD, "Education at a Glance 2011."

[10] Eurostat, "General government expenditure by function (COFOG) [gov_a_exp]," updated July 20, 2012.

[11] WDI, "Age dependency ratio, old (% of working-age population)," accessed November 2, 2012.

[12] Transparency International, *Corruption Perceptions Index 2009*.

[13] Greece's "shadow economy" was put at 25.2% of GDP in 2010, versus an EU-27 average of 21.1% of GDP. Schneider, "Size and Development of the Shadow Economy of 31 European Countries from 2003 to 2010."

[14] WEF, *The Global Competitiveness Index 2012-2013 data platform*, accessed November 3, 2012.

[15] "Globalisation and its critics," *The Economist*, September 27, 2001.

[16] Artavanis, et. al., "Tax Evasion Across Industries: Soft Credit Evidence from Greece."

[17] Eurostat, "Employment by sex, age and professional status (1 000) [lfsa_egaps]," accessed November 2, 2012.

[18] Greek Ministry of Finance, "Amesi paremvasi gia tis liksiprothesmes ofiles," July 8, 2011.

[19] Lewis, "Beware of Greeks Bearing Bonds."

[20] European Commission, "Report on Greek Government Deficit and Debt Statistics," January 2010.

[21] World Bank, *Doing Business Report 2010*.

[22] UNCTAD, Inward and outward foreign direct investment stock, annual, 1980-2011.

[23] OECD, "Indicators of regulation in energy, transport and communications (ETCR)," accessed September 24, 2012.

[24] OECD, Economic Survey of Greece 2011, 40.

25 EC, "The Economic Adjustement for Greece, Fourth review – spring 2011," 41.

26 OECD, *Economic Survey of Greece 2011*, 113.

27 Eurostat, "Employment (main characteristics and rates) - annual averages," accessed November 3, 2012.

28 OECD, "OECD Labour productivity growth in the total economy," accessed August 31, 2012.

29 Eurostat, "Monthly minimum wages - bi-annual data [earn_mw_cur]," and "GDP and main components - Current prices [nama_gdp_c],"accessed November 3, 2012.

30 Eurostat, "GDP and main components - Current prices [nama_gdp_c]," accessed November 3, 2012.

31 Simitis, *I Krisi*, 39.

32 Eurostat, "Employment by sex, age and economic activity (from 2008, NACE rev.2) (1 000) [lfsa_egan2]," accessed November 3, 2012

33 Eurostat, "National Accounts by 10 branches - aggregates at current prices [nama_nace10_c], Updated October 31, 2012.

34 Frieden, "The Euro: Who Wins? Who Loses," 30—31.

35 Quoted in Robert A. Mundell, "A Theory of Optimum Currency Areas," 662.

36 Mundell, "A Theory of Optimum Currency Areas," 662.

37 Feldstein, "EMU and International Conflict."

38 EC, "Geographical and labour market mobility, Special Eurobarometer 337, June 2010.

39 Eurostat, "Nearly two-thirds of the foreigners living in EU Member States are citizens of countries outside the EU-27," Statistics in focus 31/2012.

40 United States Census Bureau, "Lifetime Mobility in the United States: 2010."

41 Waysand, et al. "European financial linkages: A new look at imbalances."

[42] Feldstein and Horioka, "Domestic Saving and International Capital Flows," 314-329.

[43] Blanchard, and Giavazzi, "Current Account Deficits in the Euro Area. The End of the Feldstein Horioka Puzzle?"

[44] Ash, "The Crisis of Europe," 6.

[45] Feldstein, "EMU and International Conflict."

[46] Rogoff, "A euro parable: the couple with a joint account."

[47] Ash, "The Crisis of Europe," 6.

[48] Malcolm, "The Case Against 'Europe'."

[49] Krugman, "Greece as Victim."

[50] Creswell and Bowley, "Ratings Firms Misread Signs of Greek Woes."

[51] Creswell and Bowley, "Ratings Firms Misread Signs of Greek Woes."

[52] Friedman and Mundell, "One World, One Money?"

[53] Marsh, *The Euro*, 1.

[54] Weisbrot, "Why Greece Should Reject the Euro."

[55] IMF, *World Economic Outlook Database*, October 2012.

[56] The Economist, "The price of cooking the books," February 25, 2012.

[57] Transparency International, Corruption Perceptions Index 2010.

[58] Transparency International, Corruption Perceptions Index 2001.

[59] Heritage Foundation / Wall Street Journal Economic Freedom index.

[60] World Bank, *Doing Business Report 2013*, October 2012.

[61] WEF, *The Global Competitiveness Index 2012-2013 data platform*, accessed November 3, 2012.

[62] Eurostat, "Government finance statistics," accessed November 3, 2012.

[63] Eurostat, "Government finance statistics," accessed November 3, 2012.

64 Pisani-Ferry, "The Euro Crisis and the New Impossible Trinity," 17.

65 Pisani-Ferry, "The Euro Crisis and the New Impossible Trinity," 18.

66 Merler and Pisani-Ferry, "The Simple Macroeconomics of North and South in EMU."

67 World Economic Forum, *The Global Competitiveness Index 2012–2013*, 25.

68 Eurostat, "International investment position - annual data [bop_ext_intpos]," updated October 19, 2012.

69 Riegert, "Crisis topples governments like dominos."

70 Ash, "The Crisis of Europe," 6.

71 Der Spiegel Online Poll, http://www.spiegel.de/international/germany/spiegel-online-survey-germans-opposed-to-further-euro-bailouts-a-843000.html

72 Bergsten, "Why the Euro Will Survive." 17.

73 Kindleberger, *Manias, Panics and Crashes*, 10.

74 Ministry of Finance, Public Debt Bulletins No. 64 (December 2011) and No. 65 (March 2012).

75 IMF, "Greece: Request for Extended Arrangement Under the Extended Fund Facility …" 93.

76 Roubini, "Greece's Best Option is an Orderly Default."

77 IMF, "Greece: Staff Report on Request for Stand-By Arrangement." Eurostat, "Government Finance Statistics: Government deficit/surplus, debt and associated data (gov_dd_edpt1)," accessed November 5, 2012.

78 Reinhart and Roggoff, *This Time is Different*, 23–24.

79 Reinhart and Roggoff, *This Time is Different*, 120–121.

80 IMF, "Greece: Staff Report on Request for Stand-By Arrangement," 38.

81 Eurostat, "Government finance statistics," accessed November 9, 2012.

[82] IMF, "Greece: Staff Report on Request for Stand-By Arrangement," 13.

[83] Roubini, "Greece's Best Option is an Orderly Default."

[84] BIS, "Consolidated banking statistics: 9C:S Total foreign claims on ultimate risk basis (public sector)."

[85] IMF, "Greece: Staff Report on Request for Stand-By Arrangement," 27; and IMF, "Greece: Request for Extended Arrangement Under the Extended Fund Facility…," 67.

[86] Interview between George Papaconstantinou and Yanis Varoufakis, Youtube.com.

[87] IMF, "Greece: Request for Extended Arrangement Under the Extended Fund Facility …," 1.

[88] IMF, "Greece: Request for Extended Arrangement Under the Extended Fund Facility …," 6.

[89] IMF, "Greece: Request for Extended Arrangement Under the Extended Fund Facility …," 75.

[90] Friedman and Mundell, "One World, One Money," 15.

[91] Friedman and Mundell, "One World, One Money," 13.

[92] IMF, "World Economic Outlook: Recovery, Risk, and Rebalancing," 101.

[93] Eurostat, "Labour Cost Index," accessed November 10, 2012.

[94] WDI, "Official exchange rate (LCU per US$, period average)," accessed November 2, 2012.

[95] Anholt, *Places: Identity, Image and Reputation*, 4.

[96] Bauer, *From Subsistence to Exchange and Other Essays*, 6.

[97] Eurostat, "National Accounts (Including GDP), GDP and main components - Current prices (nama_gdp_c)," accessed November 6, 2012.

[98] IMF, "Greece: Request for Extended Arrangement Under the Extended Fund Facility …," 15.

[99] Eurostat, "National Accounts (Including GDP), GDP and main components - Current prices (nama_gdp_c)," ac-

cessed November 6, 2012.

[100] Kennedy, *Freedom from Fear*, 157.

[101] Alfaro, et. al., "Foreign Direct Investment and Ireland's Tiger Economy," 6..

[102] Freier, "Political Economy of the Agenda 2010 Reforms."

[103] Åslund and Dombrovskis, "How Latvia Came through the Financial Crisis," 118.

[104] Åslund and Dombrovskis, "How Latvia Came through the Financial Crisis," 4.

[105] Aslund, "Why Toomas Ilves Is Right and Paul Krugman Is Wrong."

[106] Åslund, "Why a Collapse of the Euro Area Must Be Avoided."

[107] Åslund, "Why a Breakup of the Euro Area Must Be Avoided: Lessons from Previous Breakups."

[108] Eurostat, "Unemployment in the EU27 regions," July 4, 2012.

[109] IMF, "Request for an Extended Arrangement: Ireland," December 4, 2010.

[110] IMF, "Statement by the EC, ECB, and IMF on the Review Mission to Ireland," July 12, 2012.

[111] Åslund, "Why Toomas Ilves Is Right and Paul Krugman Is Wrong."

[112] IMF, "Republic of Latvia: First Post-Program Monitoring Discussions," July 2012, p. 3.

[113] Pew Research Center, "Pervasive Gloom About the World Economy."

[114] Friedman, *Capitalism and Freedom*, ix.

[115] Friedman, *Moral Consequences of Economic Growth*, 4.

[116] Friedman, *Moral Consequences of Economic Growth*, 178.

Greece in Crisis

[1] ELSTAT, *Public Finance 2002—2006*, 40.

[2] Ministry of Finance, *Budget Execution Bulletins*, various editions.

[3] Ministry of Finance, *Budget Execution Bulletins*, various editions.

[4] Ministry of Finance, *Budget Execution Bulletins*, various editions.

[5] EC, "The Second Economic Adjustment Programme for Greece," 24; for 2011 data, I relied on the net changes reported by the Ministry of Administrative Reform.

[6] Eurostat, "General government expenditure by function (COFOG) [gov_a_exp]," Updated July 20, 2012.

[7] ELSTAT, *Statistical Yearbook of Greece*, various editions. Population over 65 from WDI, "Population ages 65 and above (% of total)."

[8] Bank of Greece, "Bulletin of Conjunctural Indicators."

[9] OECD, 17. House prices, Economics: Key Tables from OECD.

[10] Bank of Greece, "Bulletin of Conjunctural Indicators."

[11] Eurostat, "Gross fixed capital formation by 6 asset types - current prices [nama_pi6_c]," accessed November 3, 2012.

[12] Bank of Greece, "Balance of Payments."

[13] Bank of Greece, "Balance of Payments."

[14] IMF, "Greece: Second Review Under the Stand-By Arrangement ..." 52/

[15] EU Privatization Barometer.

[16] IMF, "Greece: Third Review Under the Stand-By Arrangement ..." 14.

[17] From the EU Privatization Barometer, I took every privatization from 1980 to 2009. The database includes information on 23 European countries. GDP came from the IMF World Economic Outlook (February 2010 release). For

every year, I estimated a share of privatization proceeds by merely dividing one by the other. In theory, there could be 667 observations (23 countries x 29 years). In reality, there are 397 observations, meaning that the countries in question performed no privatizations in the other years. There are, however, 7 observations where we have privatization proceeds but no GDP estimates, chiefly for former Eastern European countries where GDP numbers for the early 1990s are non-existent. So there are 390 observations in total.

[18] Ministry of Finance, National Budget 2012, November 2011, 130; National Budget 2013, October 2012, 147.

[19] Speech in Kozani, September 10, 2009; "Lefta Yparxoun an ta diekdikiseis," YouTube Video, http://www.youtube.com/watch?v=Nvg8LG3aRNw&feature=relmfu

[20] Lewis, "Beware of Greeks Bearing Bonds."

[21] IMF, "Greece: Request for Extended Arrangement Under the Extended Fund Facility …" 13.

[22] IMF, "Greece: Request for Extended Arrangement Under the Extended Fund Facility …" 48.

[23] Ministry of Interior, Electoral Results, http://ekloges.ypes.gr/, accessed May 8, 2012.

[24] Public Issue, "Greek Elections June 2012 - Voter Demographics."

[25] SYRIZA Electoral Program, as described on May18-20, 2012 on the party's website. Author's translation.

[26] Huntington, *Political Order in Changing Societies*, 347.

[27] Huntington, *Political Order in Changing Societies*, 346.

[28] Machiavelli, The Prince. Quoted in Huntington, *Political Order in Changing Societies*, 355.

[29] OECD, Greece: Review of the Central Administration, 24.

[30] Shakespeare, *Romeo and Juliet*, Act 5, Scene 1.

[31] Bank of Greece, Summary of the Annual Report 2010, April 2011, 9.

[32] Squires, "Greek 'island of the blind'? More like 'island of welfare cheats'."

[33] Public Issue, "Memorandum & Debt: One year after," Friday, May 20, 2011.

[34] Public Issue, "Memorandum & Debt: One year after: What has changed. Survey of Greek public opinion."

[35] Public Issue, "Pos Krinoun oi Ellines tis idiotikopoiseis."

Epilogue

[1] Berlin, "Fathers and Children," 296.

[2] Livingston, "Pygmalion in Management."

[3] Isaacson, "The Real Leadership Lessons of Steve Jobs."

26486514R00095

Made in the USA
Middletown, DE
30 November 2015